For You

Andreas Seidl

Handover of Power

Global Version

Volume 3: Constitution

Imprint

Bibliographic information of the German National Library: The German National Library lists this publication in the German National Bibliography; detailed bibliographic data are available on the Internet at http://dnb.dnb.de.

© 2022 Dipl. Pol. Theodor Andreas Seidl

Cover: Christiane Ebrecht
Translation: DeepL, Cologne
Production and publishing: BoD – Books on Demand, Norderstedt

ISBN: 978-3-7568-1333-9

Acknowledgements
My thanks go to my family and friends who have made me who I am today. Special thanks to all those who supported me in writing this book. I would like to thank all my classmates, teachers, fellow students, lecturers, demonstrators, activists, colleagues, companies and countries with whom I have had the privilege of sharing the experiences from which all the ideas in this book have emerged. I would like to thank the staff of Books on Demand for their kind helpfulness. I thank the citizens of Seligenstadt for the harmony and solidarity in which I was able to write.

Foreword
This policy concept contains a variety of proposals for possible political reforms. It can be peacefully and democratically adapted to any current political system of any state in the world, but also to political systems in families, clubs, associations or companies. Wherever humans make or submit to rules that manage living together, the following proposals can be helpful. Readers who find the proposals so helpful that they would like to implement them together with like-minded people can contact the author. The contact form on the last page can be used for this purpose.

Faults and defects
I ask for your understanding that this volume was not professionally proofread. I could only afford professional proofreading for the summary. Spelling errors and unfortunate phrasing may therefore occur. As soon as this volume has sold enough to pay for a professional proofreading, it will be done. After that, a new edition will be published.

English version
Please understand that this volume has been translated automatically. I could only afford a professional translation for the summary. Poor wording and spelling errors may therefore occur. In case of doubt, the German version shall prevail. As soon as this volume has sold enough to pay for a professional translation, it will be done. After that, a new edition will be

published. It was more important to me that no one in the world should have an information advantage than individual translation errors in the complete work.

References
This Constitution incorporates textual elements of the Federal Constitution of the Swiss Confederation of 18 April 1999 (as at 12 February 2017), abbreviated to BV[1] and the Constitution of the Canton of Bern of 6 June 1993 (as at 11 March 2015), abbreviated to KV[2] .
All direct quotations from the BV are *in italics*, all direct quotations from the KV are *in italics and underlined*. If the formulations in both Swiss constitutions are identical, the BV is quoted. If italicised or italicised and underlined parts of the text are interrupted by normally set parts of the text, omissions and insertions have been made by the author. Omissions are marked by (...). If words in a sentence are italicised, the rest of the sentence from which it was quoted should be compared with the content of the paragraph, because analogous indirect quotations occur through general adaptations. Similar formulations by the author are therefore neither italicised nor underlined and should be compared with the corresponding sources in the footnote. The following formulations are considered general adaptations to the Swiss constitutions: Municipality and cantons correspond to municipalities, Confederation corresponds to nation and the Federal Assembly corresponds to committee, council of ministers or party council. The Federal Council corresponds to all 18 ministers and the Federal Court to the National Court of Justice. Where state matters were meant, the term "public" was replaced by "state". Due to all the adjustments, it often happens that verbs or nouns are written in the plural in the original, but here in the singular and vice versa.
The article of the BV or KV from which the direct and indirect

---

1 This is not an official publication. Only the publication by the Swiss Federal Chancellery is authoritative. https://www.fedlex.admin.ch/eli/cc/1999/404/de On 14.12.2021
2 This is not an official publication. The Bernese Official Collection of Laws is authoritative. https://www.belex.sites.be.ch/frontend/versions/2420?locale=de#ART71 On 16.12.2021

quotations originate is listed as a footnote after the number of the paragraph. Example: §123 [Footnote: BV Art.123, KV Art.123] Sample Title [Footnote: Sample Ministry - 1.2.3 Sample Chapters]

After the title of each paragraph, a footnote refers to the volumes and chapters in which the paragraph is referred to. In the affected places in the volumes, there are also footnotes referring to the paragraph, if applicable, individual paragraphs thereof and the Swiss article(s). Example: [Footnote: §123,1,2 Sample title: BV Art.123, KV Art.123]

The formulations for persons change in the course of the communitarisation of states. In the short term, as described here, they are domestic nationals, in the medium term citizens of the united states of the continent and in the long term citizens of the earth. In the federal context, the international political level is meant for peoples, the national level for the people, and the municipal level for affected citizens. Citizens, population and those entitled to vote are used when referring to the international, national and municipal levels.

Automatic translation may result in different or incorrect wording and italicised or underlined parts may slip by a few words. The German version is authoritative.

Table of contents

Preamble[1]

In the name of humanity, the earth and the universe!
The domestic people give themselves,
in our responsibility towards creation,
striving to renew democratic unity on a daily basis in order *to strengthen* unity, justice, *freedom, democracy, independence and peace in solidarity and openness towards the world* and in the world,
in the will to live its diversity in unity in mutual consideration and respect,
aware of the common achievements and the responsibility towards future generations,
knowing that only those who use their freedom are free, and that the strength of the people is measured by the well-being of the weak,
following constitution:

Title 1: Personal rights

Chapter 1: Fundamental rights

§1[2] Human dignity[3]

The dignity of the human being must be respected and protected.

§2[4] Equality of rights[5]

1 All humans are equal before the law. Substantially equal things are to be treated equally, substantially unequal things unequally.
2 No one may be discriminated against, namely on the grounds of origin, race, gender, age, language, social status, way of life, religious, ideological or political convictions or on the grounds of

---

1 Preamble of the BV
2 BV Art.7
3 Ministry of Justice - 4.4 Proportionality, Ministry of State Organisation - 4.3.2 Fundamental rights, 8.1.3 Civil rights
4 BV Art.8
5 Ministry of Justice - 4.5 Impartiality, Ministry of State Organisation - 4.3.2 Fundamental rights, 8.1.3 Civil rights

a physical, mental or psychological disability.
3 Men and women have equal rights. The law ensures their equality in law and in fact, especially in the family, training and work. Man and woman are entitled to equal pay for work of equal value.
4 The law provides for measures to eliminate disadvantages faced by disabled persons.
5 The municipal law may provide for discriminatory exemptions in cultural protection areas.

§3[6] Protection against arbitrary state action[7]

1 *Every person has the right to be treated by the state organs without arbitrariness and* in good faith.
2 In the event of suspicion of arbitrary state action, every person has the right to report this to the police, the public prosecutor's office or Surveillance Television. The aforementioned bodies are obliged to investigate the incident and to put an end to any arbitrary rule and to punish it legally.
3 The Ministry of Justice shall determine further details in the law.

§4[8] Right to life[9]

1 *Every human being has the right to life*, but not the duty. *The death penalty is forbidden.* Suicide is permitted. Life sentenced prisoners may commit suicide at the earliest after 20 years of detention.
2 *Every human being has the right to personal freedom, in particular the right to physical and mental integrity.*
3 *Torture and any other form of cruel, inhuman or degrading treatment or punishment are prohibited.* Exceptions are such

---

6 BV Art.9
7 Ministry of Justice - 4.2 Transparency, 5.6.3.1 Charges against security agencies, Ministry of State Organisation - 4.3.2 Fundamental rights, 8.1.3 Civil rights
8 BV Art.10
9 Ministry of Justice - 4.4 Proportionality, 6.3 Suicide, 7.5.1 Restriction of rights, Ministry of Family Affairs - 11 Death, Ministry of State Organisation - 4.3.2 Fundamental rights, 8.1.3 Civil rights.

treatment for pleasure by contractually declared mutual consent.

§5[10] **Individual and social responsibility**[11]

1 Each person shall assume responsibility for him- or herself and contribute to the accomplishment of tasks in the state and society to the best of his or her ability.
2 Every person may do what he or she likes as long as he or she does not cause damage to humans or the environment.
3 Whether damage is caused to a human being is decided by that human being on a case-by-case basis, by asking permission before a potentially harmful act is carried out, whether the act may be carried out with him or her.

§6 **Moral obligations**[12]

1 Humans are there to make other humans happy.
2 Every human being may live as he or she wishes, as long as he or she does not demand that anyone else do the same. If one is damaged by the behaviour of others, one must make this known and justify it on the basis of law. But if other people's behaviour only disturbs you because you want them to behave the way you behave, you should let them live that way.
3 All humans are equal. Every human being is our species, which must be protected and preserved.
4 The most effective idea wins, no matter who it comes from or where it comes from.
5 Special situations require special measures.
6 The earth is our homeland. Its integrity until the universe destroys it is the human's highest commandment.
7 Ignorance must not be exploited and does not protect against sentence.

---

10 BV Art.6
11 Ministry of Family Affairs - 4 Manners, Ministry of State Organisation - 4.3.2 Fundamental Rights, 8.1.3 Civil Rights
12 Ministry of Family Affairs - 4 Manners, Ministry of State Organisation - 4.3.2 Fundamental Rights, 8.1.3 Civil Rights

§7[13] **Personal rights**[14]

1 All persons within the country enjoy the protection of their fundamental rights by the domestic authorities and by all their fellow citizens.
2 Every person shall *fulfil duties imposed on him or her by the Constitution and legislation based thereon.*
3 In addition to responsibility *for oneself, every person bears responsibility towards fellow human beings and co-responsibility for ensuring that the right to self-determination is also safeguarded for future generations.*
4 Every person has the lifelong right to sexual self-determination. Sexual acts with other persons require the mutual consent of all participants. Restrictions for minors are regulated by the Ministry of Family Affairs in the law.

§8[15] **Protection of children and youths**[16]

1 Children and youths are entitled to special protection of their integrity and to promotion of their development.
2 They shall exercise their rights within their capacity of judgement. They shall be democratically involved in decisions about them. They shall have the right to vote for the ministries of family and education from the age of ten.

§9[17] **Right to assistance in emergency situations**[18]

1 Anyone *in distress (...) is entitled to assistance* until his life is out of danger and he is again in possession of his physical and mental faculties.

---

13 KV Art.8
14 Ministry of Justice - 4.8 Areas of law, Ministry of State Organisation - 4.3.2 Fundamental rights, 8.1.3 Civil rights, Ministry of Family Affairs - 7.3 Partnering
15 BV Art.11
16 Ministry of Family Affairs - 7.6 Youth Welfare Office , Ministry of State Organisation - 4.3.2 Fundamental rights , 8.1.3 Civil rights
17 BV Art.12
18 Ministry of Security - 5 Prevention of danger, 6.4.1 Social intervention, Ministry of Planned Economy - 17 Social policy, Ministry of State Organisation - 4.3.2 Fundamental rights, 8.1.3 Civil rights

2 Domestic nationals who are *unable* to care for *themselves* are entitled *to assistance and care and to the means essential for a dignified existence.*

§10[19] Protection of privacy[20]

1 Every person has the right to respect for his or her private and family life, his or her home and his or her correspondence, post and telecommunications.
2 Every person is entitled to protection against misuse of their personal data.
3 Personal data is the property of the person and can only be lent with that person's consent.

§11[21] Right to marriage and family[22]

1 The *right to marriage and family is guaranteed.*
2 Any number of humans of any sex may enter into marriage and found a family.

§12[23] Freedom of belief and conscience[24]

1 Freedom of faith and conscience is guaranteed.
2 Every person has the right freely to choose and to manifest, alone or in community with others, his or her religion or belief.
3 Every person has the right to join or belong to a religious community and to follow religious instruction.
4 No one may be compelled to join or belong to a religious

---

19 BV Art.13
20 Ministry of Digital Affairs - 7 Digital data protection, 7.4 Access rights, Ministry of Justice - 8.13.3 Duty of security agencies to provide information, Ministry of Security - 6.4 Patrol service for the police including social deployment, 7.3 Digital police files, Ministry of State Organisation - 4.3.2 Fundamental rights, 8.1.3 Civil rights
21 BV Art.14
22 Ministry of Family Affairs - 6 Registry Office   , 7 Families, Ministry of State Organisation - 4.3.2 Fundamental rights, 8.1.3 Civil rights
23 BV Art.15
24 Ministry of Integration - 6.4 Religious communities, Ministry of State Organisation - 4.3.2 Fundamental rights, 8.1.3 Civil rights

community, to perform a religious act or to follow religious instruction.

§13[25] Freedom of expression and information[26]

1 Freedom of expression and information is guaranteed.
2 Everyone has the right to form his or her opinion freely and to express and disseminate it without interference.
3 Every person has the right to freely receive, obtain from generally accessible sources and disseminate information.
4 *Pre-censorship* is not *permitted in any case.*
5 Nationals have the right to *inspect* all *official files, unless there are overriding* state *or private interests to the contrary. Every person has the right to inspect* all state files concerning him or her, except for criminal investigation files of ongoing proceedings.

§14[27] Data protection[28]

1 The originator of data is the owner of that data. Data shall be considered as on loan from the originator to the user. The purpose of use must be contractually agreed. Users of this data are obliged to ensure data protection.
2 *Every person has the right to access data processed about them and to request that inaccurate data be corrected and that inappropriate or unnecessary data be destroyed.*
3 Authorities *may only process personal data if there is a legal basis for doing so and the data is suitable and necessary for the performance of their duties.*
4 *They make sure that the processed data is correct, secure it against misuse* and inform the owner about the retrieval of his data.

---

25 BV Art.16, KV Art.17
26 Ministry of Digital Affairs - 4 Digital Law, 7.3 Storage Locations, Ministry of State Organisation - 4.3.2 Fundamental Rights, 8.1.3 Civil Rights
27 KV Art.18
28 Ministry of Digital Affairs - 4 Digital Law, 7 Digital Data Protection, 7.5 Access Directory, Ministry of State Organisation - 4.3.2 Fundamental Rights, 8.1.3 Civil Rights

§15[29] Freedom of the media[30]

1 The freedom of the press, radio and television and other forms of (...) dissemination of performances and information by telecommunications shall be guaranteed.
2 Censorship is prohibited.
3 Editorial secrecy is guaranteed.
4 State media are unfree, beholden to the law and the people, and operated by the ministries of media and digital.

§16[31] Language freedom[32]

1 *Freedom of language is guaranteed.* Persons may speak the language they prefer.
2 In language and correspondence with state institutions and employees, the domestic language shall be the official language.

§17[33] Right to education and research[34]

1 The right *to sufficient and free* education and its rating by the taught *is guaranteed* for life for all domestic nationals by the Ministry of Education.
2 The right to support research and development is guaranteed for life for all domestic nationals by the Ministry of Innovation.

---

29 BV Art.17
30 Ministry of Media Affairs - 4 Media Affairs , Ministry of State Organisation - 4.3.2 Fundamental Rights, 8.1.3 Civil Rights
31 BV Art.18
32 Ministry of Integration - 6.1 Official languages, Ministry of State Organisation - 4.3.2 Fundamental rights, 8.1.3 Civil rights
33 BV Art.19
34 Ministry of Education - 4 Education system, Ministry of Innovation - 5 Research and development, Ministry of State Organisation - 4.3.2 Fundamental rights, 8.1.3 Civil rights

§18[35] Academic freedom[36]

1 The freedom of academic teaching and research is guaranteed.
<u>*2 Persons engaged in science, research and teaching shall assume their responsibility towards the integrity of human, animal and plant life and their life-support systems.*</u>

§19[37] Freedom of art[38]

1 The freedom of art is guaranteed.
2 Art must operate within the framework of this constitution.
3 The Ministry of Family Affairs shall lay down more detailed provisions on the definition of art in the law.

§20[39] Freedom of assembly[40]

1 Freedom of assembly is guaranteed.
2 Every person has the right to organise meetings, to attend meetings or to stay away from meetings.
3 Demonstrations <u>*on public property may be declared subject to authorisation by law (...). They shall be permitted if an orderly process is ensured and the disturbance of other users appears reasonable.*</u>
4 The Ministry of Security shall determine more detailed provisions on reasonable interference in the law.

---

35 BV Art.20, KV Art.21
36 Ministry of Education - 4.1 Scientific freedom, Ministry of Innovation - 5 Research and Development, Ministry of State Organisation - 4.3.2 Fundamental Rights, 8.1.3 Civil Rights
37 BV Art.21
38 Ministry of Family Affairs - 9.1 Arts, Ministry of State Organisation - 4.3.2 Fundamental rights , 8.1.3 Civil rights
39 BV Art.22, KV Art.19
40 Ministry of Security - 4.8 Large Events, 4.9 Demonstrations, Ministry of State Organisation - 4.3.2 Fundamental Rights, 8.1.3 Civil Rights

§21[41] **Freedom of association**[42]

1 Freedom of association is guaranteed.
2 Every person has the right to form, join or belong to clubs and to participate in the activities of unifications.
3 No one may be forced to join or belong to a unification.

§22 **Freedom of movement**[43]

1 Every person may move freely within the inland without fear for his or her physical, mental and financial integrity.
2 In cultural protection areas, the first violation of the exemption rule there must be punished with a warning. The second offence is punishable by a dismissal, which extends to the entire cultural protection area.
3 More detailed provisions on cultural protection areas shall be determined by the Ministry of Integration in the law.

§23[44] **Freedom of establishment**[45]

1 Nationals *have the right to* settle anywhere in *the country.*
2 The place may be restricted by law in a cultural protection area.
3 Domestic citizens *have the right to leave or* enter the inland.
4 The Ministry of Integration shall determine more detailed provisions for foreigners in the law.

---

41 BV Art.23
42 Ministry of Family Affairs - 9.6 Clubs, Ministry of State Organisation - 4.3.2 Fundamental Rights, 8.1.3 Civil Rights
43 Ministry of Integration - 4.4 Residents' Registration Office, 6.3 Cultural Protection Area, Ministry of State Organisation - 4.3.2 Fundamental Rights, 8.1.3 Civil Rights
44 BV Art.24
45 Ministry of Integration - 4.4 Residents' Registration Office, 7 Immigration, Ministry of State Organisation - 4.3.2 Fundamental Rights, 8.1.3 Civil Rights

§24[46] Protection against expulsion, extradition and deportation[47]

1 Domestic citizens *may not be expelled from* the inland.
2 *They may only be extradited to a foreign authority with their consent* or by order of a domestic court following its final judgement.
3 Foreigners may not *be* deported *or extradited to a state where they are persecuted* or where they are *threatened with torture or any other kind of cruel and inhuman treatment or punishment.*
4 Foreigners lose this right if they break this constitution by committing criminal offences inland. The offenders must have been sentenced to imprisonment or 3 lesser sentences by domestic courts. The departure must take place directly after serving the imprisonment.
5 More detailed provisions on foreigners are set out in the law by the Ministry of Integration.

§25[48] Property guarantee[49]

1 Ownership is guaranteed.
2 Expropriations and restrictions on ownership that amount to an expropriation shall be fully compensated.
3 Property must be disposed of in a professional manner without causing damage to humans and nature. The appropriation of disposed property is permissible for everyone until the disposal company commissioned by the disposing owner can take possession of the property. If other humans wish to continue using the disposed property, it becomes their property.
4 Municipalities *create favourable conditions for the broad distribution of private land ownership, especially for self-use and*

---

46 BV Art.25
47 Ministry of Foreign Affairs - 4.7.3 Embassies for countries, Ministry of Integration - 7.9.3 Deportation, Ministry of Justice - 2.4.2.1 Extradition requests, 8.9.4 Deportations, Ministry of State Organisation - 4.3.2 Fundamental rights, 8.1.3 Civil rights
48 BV Art.26, KV Art.24
49 Ministry of Labour - 9.2 Property, 20.7.6.12 Implementation of expropriation, Ministry of Infrastructure - 4.4.1 Housing, Ministry of State Organisation - 4.3.2 Fundamental rights, 8.1.3 Civil rights.

self-management by domestic nationals.

§26[50] Economic freedom[51]

1 Full economic freedom *is guaranteed* in the Free Market Economy and is only limited by the Constitution and the Ministries of Labour and Free Market Economy. Economic freedom is restricted in the Barter Economy, Social Market Economy and Planned Economy by the responsible Ministry of Economy.
2 The freedom of election to a profession *and to a job, economic activity and the right to professional and labour union association* are *guaranteed* for nationals and migrant workers.
3 *It includes in particular the free election* for capital and labour between the four economic forms, the profession, *as well as the free admission to an economic gainful activity and its free and safe exercise.*
4 The four economic forms offer different conditions for freedom and security in poverty or wealth in risk and money.
a. Free and poor are members of the Barter Economy.
b. Safe and poor are members of the Planned Economy.
c. Secure and rich are members of the social market economy.
d. Free and rich are members of the Free Market Economy.
5 The ministries of economy shall issue regulations on freedom of contract.
6 The ministries of Labour, Barter Economy, Planned Economy, Social Market Economy and Free Market Economy enact more detailed provisions on the design of the four economic forms in the law.

---

50 BV Art.27, KV Art.23
51 Ministry of Labour - 10 Freedom of movement between economic forms, Ministry of State Organisation - 4.3.2 Fundamental rights, 8.1.3 Civil rights

§27 Common good[52]

1 The common good is defined by the people in this article of the constitution.
2 Citizens are consulted in a constitutional committee about which basic needs are most important to them.
3 The currently valid common good is described in the fundamental rights.
4 The rights of freedom may be limited by the common good, in particular economic freedom.
5 Economic freedom can be restricted to different degrees by the common good in different economic forms. Basic restrictions affecting all economic forms are laid down by the Ministry of Labour in the law.

§28[53] Freedom of coalition[54]

1 Workers, employers and their organisations shall have the right to unite for the protection of their interests, to form clubs and to join or to stay away from such clubs.
2 Wherever possible, disputes shall be settled by negotiation or mediation.
3 Strikes and lock-outs are permitted if they affect industrial relations and if there are no conflicting obligations to maintain industrial peace or to conduct conciliation negotiations.
4 The law may prohibit certain categories of occupational groups from striking. Compensatory measures shall be determined by the affected citizens in a committee.

52Ministry of Labour - 10 Freedom of movement between economic forms, 20.7.3.2 Private sector audit, 20.7.6.2 Constitutional law audit, Ministry of State Organisation - 4.3.2 Fundamental rights, 8.1.3 Civil rights
53BV Art.28
54Ministry of Labour - 16.7 Industrial action, Ministry of State Organisation - 4.3.2 Fundamental rights, 8.1.3 Civil rights

§29[55] General procedural guarantees[56]

1 In proceedings before judicial and administrative bodies, every person has the right to equal and fair treatment and to be judged within a reasonable *time.*
2 The parties shall have the right to be heard.
3 Domestic citizens who do not have *the necessary means are entitled to free legal assistance if their legal claim does not appear to be futile. To the extent necessary to safeguard their rights, nationals* are also entitled to free *legal assistance.*

§30[57] Judicial proceedings[58]

1 Every person whose case is subject to judicial proceedings shall be entitled to a court established by law which is competent, independent and impartial. Courts of exception are prohibited.
2 Any person against whom a civil action is brought is entitled to have the matter heard by the court of his or her place of residence. The law may provide for a different place of jurisdiction.
3 Court hearings and pronouncements of judgement are public. They are published permanently by state media. Exceptions are possible in the case of minors. Anonymisation of the faces and the votes of plaintiffs and defendants are permissible at the request of those affected.
4 In all proceedings, the parties shall have the right to be heard, to inspect the files, to a reasoned court judgment within a reasonable *period of time, and to a notice of appeal.*
5 Every person shall be presumed *innocent until finally convicted in a court of law. In case of doubt, the decision shall be in favour of the* accused.

---

55 BV Art.29
56 Ministry of Justice - 5 court proceedings, 5.6 court staff, Ministry of State Organisation - 4.3.2 fundamental rights, 8.1.3 civil rights
57 BV Art.30, KV Art.26
58 Ministry of Justice - 4.8.1 Civil law, 5 Court proceedings, 5.4 Courts, Ministry of State Organisation - 4.3.2 Fundamental rights, 8.1.3 Civil rights

§31[59] Legal protection[60]

1 Every person has an inalienable right to (...) elected, *impartial judges provided by law.*
2 All costs for court proceedings are pre-financed by the Ministry of Justice.
3 All proceedings in sentence and constitutional law are financed by value added tax.
4 All proceedings in civil and state law are financed through legal expenses insurance or independently.
5 Additional remuneration for legal counsels is only permitted in the Free Market Economy.

§32[61] Deprivation of liberty[62]

1 A person may be deprived of his or her liberty only in the cases provided for by the law itself and only in the manner prescribed by the law.

2 Every person deprived of his or her liberty shall have the right to be informed promptly and in a language which he or she understands of the reasons for the deprivation of liberty and of his or her rights. He or she must have the opportunity to assert his or her rights. In particular, he or she has the right to have his or her next of kin notified.

3 Every person who is taken into pre-trial detention has the right to be brought before a judge without delay. The judge shall decide whether the person shall continue to be held in detention or be released. Every person in pre-trial detention is entitled to a judgment within a reasonable time.

4 Every person who is not deprived of his or her liberty by a court has the right to appeal to a court at any time. The court shall decide as soon as possible on the lawfulness of the deprivation of liberty.

---

59 KV Art.26
60 Ministry of Justice - 5.6.1 Judges, 5.7 Financing, 5.7.7 Legal expenses insurance, Ministry of State Organisation - 4.3.2 Fundamental rights, 8.1.3 Civil rights
61 BV Art.31, KV Art.25
62 Ministry of Justice - 4.8.2 criminal law, 5 court proceedings, 5.6 court staff, 7.5 detention, Ministry of State Organisation - 4.3.2 fundamental rights, 8.1.3 civil rights

5 *Every person who has been deprived of liberty shall have the right:*
a. to consult a legal adviser (...);
b. to have the deprivation of liberty reviewed in a simple and speedy judicial procedure.
6 If *the deprivation of liberty proves to be unlawful or unjustified, the community shall owe the person affected full compensation for the damage (...).*

§33[63] Criminal proceedings[64]

1 Every accused person has the right to be informed as quickly and comprehensively as possible of the charges against him or her. He or she must have the opportunity to assert the rights of defence to which he or she is entitled.
2 Every convicted person has the right to have the sentence reviewed by a higher court until the highest court is reached.

§34[65] Right of petition[66]

1 Domestic citizens have *the right to petition* state agencies *and collect signatures without suffering disadvantages.*
2 Restrictions on the right to submit individual petitions shall not be permitted under any circumstances.
3 Petitions have a term of 2 weeks, during which no minimum number of supporters is required. Petitions must be examined *and answered* by the responsible body *within* 6 months after expiry.
4 Petitions can consist of praise, factual criticism and suggestions for improvement. They are to be understood as suggestions by citizens for citizens in the state service.
5 Petitions can also be signature lists for initiatives. The duration and examination of the petition remain unchanged.

---

63 BV Art.32
64 Ministry of Justice - 5 Court Proceedings, Ministry of State Organisation - 4.3.2 Fundamental Rights, 8.1.3 Civil Rights
65 KV Art.20
66 Ministry of State Organisation - 9.10.11.6 Petition, Ministry of State Organisation - 4.3.2 Fundamental rights, 8.1.3 Civil rights

All supporters of the petition automatically give their vote for the current initiative quorum with their signature.

§35[67] Political rights[68]

1 Political rights are guaranteed for citizens within the framework of dynamic media democracy.
2 The guarantee of political rights protects the free formation of will and the undistorted casting of votes.
3 The ministries of state organisation, media and digital provide goods and services to citizens to exercise political rights.

§36[69] Realisation of fundamental rights[70]

1 Fundamental rights must be given validity throughout the legal system.
2 Anyone who performs state functions is bound by fundamental rights and obliged to contribute to their realisation.
3 The authorities shall ensure that fundamental rights, insofar as they are capable of doing so, are also effective among private individuals.

§37 Cultural protection areas[71]

1 Discriminatory laws may apply in cultural protection areas and restrict fundamental rights.
2 Conduct may be determined to be inadmissible or exclusive,

---

67 BV Art.34
68 Ministry of State Organisation - 9.2 Political rights, Ministry of Digital Affairs - 4 Digital rights, 13 People's Innovation Company Intranet, Ministry of Media Affairs - 5.7 Interactivity, Ministry of State Organisation - 4.3.2 Fundamental rights, 8.1.3 Civil rights.
69 BV Art.35
70 Ministry of Justice - 8 Criminal Law of Ministries, Ministry of State Organisation - 4.3.2 Fundamental Rights, 8.1.3 Civil Rights
71 Ministry of State Organisation - 11.5.7 Cultural protection areas for the protection of minorities, Ministry of Integration - 6.3 Cultural protection area, Ministry of State Organisation - 4.3.2 Fundamental rights, 8.1.3 Civil rights

or persons with certain characteristics may be excluded from permanent residence.

3 Special laws, conduct and features shall be posted on the town entrance sign.

4 Visitors of residents or transients who do not comply with the requirements may enter the cultural protection area for as long as necessary.

5 The right to physical, material and financial integrity shall always be granted to every human being. It may only be restricted by the ministries of security and justice in the event of violations of the law.

6 Cultural protection areas may be dissolved by the Minister of Integration and the people if they endanger public safety or spread excessively.

7 The Ministry of Integration shall regulate further details on the formation, existence and dissolution in the law.

§38[72] Restrictions on fundamental rights[73]

1 Restrictions on fundamental rights require a lawful basis. The content, purpose and scope must be sufficiently determined.
2 The foregoing is reserved for cases of serious, imminent and obvious danger, in particular where the lives and health of humans, the exercise of democratic rights or irreparable damage to the environment are at stake.
3 Restrictions on fundamental rights must be justified by a public interest or by the protection of fundamental rights of third parties.
4 Restrictions on fundamental rights must be proportionate.
5 The core content of fundamental rights is inviolable. The core content includes, in particular, guarantees which this constitution designates as inviolable or in respect of which it does not permit any restrictions under any circumstances.

---

72 BV Art.36, KV Art.28
73 Ministry of Security - 4.1 Security forces, Ministry of State Organisation - 4.3.2 Fundamental rights, 8.1.3 Civil rights

Chapter 2: Civil and political rights

§39[74] Civil rights[75]

1 A national with national civil rights *is a person who has national* citizenship.
2 Domestic nationals have international, national and municipal electoral and voting rights. They also enjoy the protection and care of state services. They are accorded the rights and duties guaranteed by law.
3 Foreigners living permanently inland who have been naturalised have electoral and voting rights for statistical purposes in order to promote harmonious coexistence and avoid parallel societies.
4 No one may be favoured *or disadvantaged because of their civil rights.*

§40[76] Acquisition and loss of civil rights[77]

1 The Ministry of Integration regulates the *acquisition and loss of civil rights by descent, marriage and adoption.* It also regulates the loss *of (...) civil rights for other reasons as well as re-naturalisation.*
2 It shall issue regulations on the number of naturalisations and stays of foreigners in the inland or the municipality *and shall issue the naturalisation permit.*

§41[78] Exercise of political rights[79]

1 The Ministry of State Organisation *regulates the exercise of political rights in* international, national *and municipal affairs.*

---

74 BV Art.37
75 Ministry of State Organisation - 8.1.3 Civil rights
76 BV Art.38
77 Ministry of Integration - 4.2 Foreigners, 4.3 Changes of status
78 BV Art.39
79 Ministry of Digital Affairs - 7 Digital data protection, 11 Intranet, Ministry of Media Affairs - 5 State broadcasting, 5.7 Interactivity, 5.7.3 Vox Pop Box, 7 Government Television, Ministry of State Organisation - 9.2 Political rights

2 Political rights are exercised in public places, in the town hall and on the intranet.
3 No one may exercise political rights in more than one municipality.
4 The Ministry of Media Affairs shall ensure the broadcasting of opinion-forming events on state television and the opportunities for those entitled to vote to participate.
5 The Ministry of Digital Affairs ensures the technical participation possibilities to be able to exercise political rights nationwide at any time. Data security and data protection are guaranteed.

§42[80] Nationals living abroad[81]

1 The Ministry of Foreign Affairs *promotes relations among nationals living abroad.*
2 It shall issue *regulations on the rights and duties of nationals living abroad, namely with regard to the exercise of national* or municipal political *rights (...), the fulfilment of the duty to perform People's Service, as well as any* social security contributions.

Chapter 3: Social rights

§43[82] Social rights[83]

1 Domestic nationals are entitled *to shelter, the means necessary for a dignified life and basic medical care in times of need.*
2 Every child shall have the right to protection, care and attention, and to free education appropriate to his or her abilities.
3 Victims of serious crimes are entitled to assistance in overcoming their difficulties.
4 In the short term, only domestic citizens are entitled to social rights; in the medium term, foreigners from countries that are in an International Union with the inland and have

---

80 BV Art.40
81 Ministry of Foreign Affairs - 4.7.3.2 Stay abroad
82 KV Art.29
83 Ministry of Planned Economy - 6.1 Entrance to Planned Economy, 18.1.7 Children's Home

communitarised social rights are also entitled. In the long term, social rights should be available to all humans in the united states of the world.

§44[84] Social welfare[85]

1 The Ministry of Planned Economy provides for needy domestics in its Social Villages.
2 They promote prevention and self-help, combat the causes of poverty and prevent social hardship.

§45[86] Welfare state[87]

1 The ministries of Planned Economy, Health, *Education* and *Infrastructure, in addition to personal responsibility and private initiative, are committed that:*
a. all domestic nationals participate in *social security;*
b. all nationals receive *the care necessary for their health;*
c. Families as communities of adults and children are protected and promoted;
d. employable people are able to earn a living by working under decent conditions;
e. Housing seekers are able to find adequate housing for themselves and their family on affordable terms;
f. children and youths as well as employable people can educate, train and develop themselves according to their abilities;
g. Children and youths are encouraged in their development as independent and socially responsible persons and supported in their social, cultural and political integration.
2 The Ministry of Planned Economy ensures that all nationals are protected *against the economic consequences of old age,* disability, *illness, accident, unemployment, homelessness,*

---

84 KV Art.38
85 Ministry of Planned Economy - 17.1 Social welfare
86 BV Art.41
87 Ministry of Planned Economy - 16.3.4 Compensation, 17 Social policy, 18.1.8 Education Centre, Ministry of Health - 5.12 Health insurance, 6 Health prevention, Ministry of Education - 5.3 School law, 5.5 Children and youths, Ministry of Infrastructure - 5.13 Housebuilding programme

parenthood, *orphanhood and widowhood.* To this end, it maintains Social Villages where Planned Economy prevails.

3 Ministries shall implement *social rights within their constitutional responsibilities and available resources.*

4 The ministries for Social Market Economy and Free Market Economy pay for the expansion of Social Villages if expansion is necessary due to increased unemployment in the respective economic form.

5 More detailed provisions on Social Villages are set out in the law by the Ministry of Planned Economy.

Title 2: State organisation

Chapter 1: State foundations

§46[88] State[89]

1 The state consists of all ministries, their capital and employees.

2 The Ministry of State Organisation ensures the functional cooperation between ministries and citizens as well as the moderation of state and policy meetings of several ministries or levels.

3 All ministries focus their actions on running the state in an entrepreneurially efficient and constitutionally stable manner in the long term.

4 The ministries of labour and economy give citizens the opportunity to choose between four economic forms in order to find their own level of freedom or security.

5 The ministries of state organisation, digital affairs and media are responsible for making the state dynamically more or less directly democratically controllable for its citizens.

6 The Ministry of State Organisation also deals with *business*

---

88 BV Art.173

89 Ministry of Digital Affairs - 2.1.2.1 Digital Service, Ministry of Media Affairs - 5 State Broadcasting, Ministry of State Organisation - 4.1 State Procedural Law, 4.1.1 Lack of Responsibility, 4.4 Federal Moderator's Office, 5.3 Theory of the State as an Economic Entrepreneur, 8.4 Ministries, 9.1 Dynamic Democracy, 9.5.11 Participation Quorum, 9.7.6 Annual Budget Vote, 10.4 Subsidiarity Agency

that falls within the responsibility of the State *and is not assigned to any other agency.*

§47 People[90]

1 All domestic nationals form the domestic people and lead their state together as a nation. In the medium term, all continental nationals form the continental people, and in the long term, all the people form a nation which shall jointly give itself a constitution by direct democratic voting.
2 The people make all decisions at the national level. Citizens can either be active only at the national level or can also join together as affected citizens by municipality, area or issue to form a community below the national level to make decisions at the municipal level.

§48 Citizens affected[91]

1 All domestic citizens affected by a policy are considered affected citizens.
2 In individual cases, these can be citizens of a municipality or citizens affected by a state, corporate or cultural policy.
3 citizens, can claim to be affected if at least 5000 citizens are affected in the same or very similar way, thereby triggering a quorum.
4 The Ministry of State Organisation shall determine further details in a law.

§49[92] Purpose[93]

1 The people shall *protect the freedom and rights of the people and preserve the independence and security of the country.*
2 It shall *promote the common welfare, sustainable development, internal cohesion and cultural diversity of the country.*
3 It ensures the greatest possible equality of opportunity

90 Ministry of State Organisation - 8.1 Domestic nationals, 8.1.1 People
91 Ministry of State Organisation - 8.1.2 Affected citizens
92 BV Art.2
93 Ministry of State Organisation - 8.1.1 People

among citizens.

4 It is committed to the *permanent preservation of the natural foundations of life and to a peaceful and just international order.*

§50[94] Nation[95]

1 *The nation* is sovereign *insofar as its sovereignty is not limited by the* constitution.

2 It exercises *all the rights conferred on* it by the people in voting and forms the national level of the state.

3 It may surrender rights to the individual municipality or several municipalities in the alliance by means of a subsidiarity vote.

4 The Ministry of State Organisation shall determine further details in the law.

§51[96] Municipalities[97]

1 Municipalities *are sovereign insofar as their sovereignty is not limited by the constitution* or the nation.

2 *They exercise all rights that* the citizens of a municipality wish to administer themselves and which, in the spirit of subsidiarity, can be better administered municipally than nationally or internationally.

3 The ministries of security and justice cannot be part of municipal self-government.

§52[98] Subsidiarity[99]

1 *The principle of subsidiarity shall be observed in the allocation and fulfilment of state tasks.*

2 The nation and municipalities can have the people determine the responsibilities for exercising the rights of individual

---

94 BV Art.3
95 Ministry of State Organisation - 8.1.1 People, 10.3 Subsidiarity Voting
96 BV Art.3
97 Ministry of State Organisation - 11.5.1 Municipality
98 BV Art.5a
99 Ministry of State Organisation - 8.1.1 People, 10 Subsidiarity

ministries by subsidiarity vote.

3 The Ministry of State Organisation shall determine further details in the law.

§53 National language[100]

The national language is the language spoken by most domestic citizens in the inland.

§54[101] Principles of the rule of law[102]

1 The basis and barrier of state action is the law.
2 State action must be in the public interest and proportionate.
3 State organs and private persons shall act in accordance with the Constitution to the best of their knowledge and belief.
4 Nation and municipalities observe international law.
5 Debt is always borne by a person or a generation. The inheritance of guilt is inadmissible.
6 A *conviction for an act or omission which was not a criminal offence at the time it was committed shall not be admissible in any case.*

§55 Communitarisation of states[103]

1 All states form a long-term alliance and all the peoples jointly adopt a constitution by direct democratic voting.

2 All provisions of this constitution that are designated by name as "domestic" change the name in the course of a communitarisation to the name of the new federal state.

3 All civic rights of the Constitution apply to all nationals of the communitarised states.

4 All humans who wish to discriminately care for their folklore can do so in the form of cultural protection areas within the former national borders.

---

100 Ministry of State Organisation - 4.1.4 National language
101 BV Art.5, KV Art.26
102 Ministry of Justice - 4.1 Predictability, 4.3 Legal certainty
103 Ministry of Foreign Affairs - 5.8.2.3 Inner Ring, 5.8.2.3.1 Constitutional Negotiations

5 All affected citizens of all affected states must agree to the communitarisation of their states in a direct democratic voting with a majority of 90%.

Chapter 2: Parties

§56[104] Political parties[105]

1 The political parties participate in the formation of the opinion and will of the people.
2 They provide the personnel of the state.
3 They design programmes for their ministry.
4 They accompany legislative and decision-making processes of their ministry through advice to citizens, participation in committees and the exercise of borrowed voting rights of citizens.
5 There is one party per ministry with a basic programme describing the subject area.
6 Parties have any number of party wings and represent different opinions and solutions in them.
7 Party donations are permissible. Timings, amounts and donors must be published on state television and stored on the intranet. Party donations shall flow equally to all party wings.

§57 Party members[106]

1 All domestic nationals may be members of any number of parties.
2 Free entry and exit is guaranteed at all times.
3 Membership fees are not permitted.

---

104 BV Art.137
105 Ministry of State Organisation - 8.5 Parties
106 Ministry of State Organisation - 8.5.5 Party membership, 8.6.4.4 Delegates

§58[107] Parliamentary groups[108]

1 *The members* of a party wing or several party wings of a party *may form parliamentary groups* within the councils.
2 There must be at least two parliamentary groups of one party.
3 There shall be no factional compulsion.

Chapter 3: Government personnel

§59 Politicians[109]

1 Politicians are all persons whose employment contract with the state has come about through an election and can be terminated by a deselection quorum.
2 Politicians are, by name, ministers, deputy ministers and popularly elected executives of a ministry.

§60[110] Eligibility[111]

1 All party members may stand for election of persons as politicians and *are eligible to vote for all those entitled to vote.*
2 The people shall determine the eligibility of all officers of ministries at the national level.
3 The citizens of the municipalities determine the eligibility of all municipal responsible ministry employees.
4 A quorum of 25% is sufficient to trigger the eligibility of a person in the state service.
5 A quorum of 75% is sufficient to exclude the eligibility of a person in the state service.

---

107 BV Art.154
108 Ministry of State Organisation - 8.6.1 Parliamentary groups
109 Ministry of State Organisation - 8.3 politicians, 9.9 election of persons
110 BV Art.143
111 Ministry of State Organisation - 9.5.12 Staff quorum, 9.9.4.7 Candidates, 9.9.4.8 Candidates' committee

§61 Election of persons process[112]

1 All politicians within a ministry are directly elected. Political staff is sent by the party of the respective ministry.

2 Citizens who are affected by the elections of political personnel directly elect these politicians. Politicians occupy specific offices within ministries that are determined by the population to be politically relevant and are thus directly elected. Directly elected politicians include at least the ministers and deputy ministers of all municipalities.

3 The election procedure shall be carried out by the ministries of state organisation, media and digital affairs together with the affected ministry in voting with the affected citizens. The Ministry of Media Affairs shall regulate in the law the details of the interactive format of the staff election, which shall ensure participation opportunities for all those entitled to vote.[113]

4 party wings express their attitudes and intentions in programmes. All party wings present their different programmes during the election campaign. They present their programmes to the citizens for pre-election.

5 The pre-election identifies the most popular programmes. After the pre-election, committees decide what can be combined from which programmes, what will be deleted and what is incompatible. Several programmes may be up for run-off election and which candidate should be responsible for them.

6 All candidates compete after the pre-election to prove their qualification for the office.

7 In a run-off election, all candidates who can reconcile the implementation of a programme from the pre-election with their conscience will stand for election.

8 The timing of a new election depends on the deselection quorum of the responsible politicians.

9 The Ministry of State Organisation shall lay down more detailed provisions on the deselection quorum in the law.

---

112 Ministry of State Organisation - 9.9 Election of persons, 9.9.4 Procedure, 9.9.4.8 Candidates' committee
113 Ministry of Media Affairs - 7.2.3.1 Election of persons committees

§62[114] Incompatibilities[115]

1 Politicians *may not hold* more than one office at the same time and may not engage in any *other gainful activity.*
2 *The law may provide for further incompatibilities.*

§63[116] Term of office[117]

1 The new election is held according to the deselection quorum. As soon as a percentage of citizens set at the election vote in favour of the deselection of a politician during an unlimited period of time, the quorum is triggered.
2 All those entitled to vote have one vote per politician for the deselection quorum. Those entitled to vote are free to decide when they cast their vote.
3 politicians are eligible to stand for re-election. There must be at least 2 other candidates in this election.

§64[118] Public liability[119]

1 Politicians are liable *for damage that* they and their *organs cause unlawfully in the exercise of official activities.*
2 Official liability may result in the loss of the office and ordinary criminal proceedings.
3 *The law shall define liability in other cases. It regulates the responsibility of the authorities and government personnel.*
4 The Ministry of State Organisation shall *determine* in the law *under which conditions the* state shall *also be liable for damage caused by its organs through lawful action.*

---

114 BV Art.144
115 Ministry of State Organisation - 9.9.3 Incompatibilities
116 BV Art.145
117 Ministry of State Organisation - 9.9.2 Term of office
118 BV Art.146, KV Art.71
119 Ministry of Justice - 8.14.2.1 Public liability

§65[120] **Instruction ban**[121]

1 Politicians and citizens vote *without instructions.* Politicians are only bound by the will of the people and applicable laws.
2 Instructions may only play a role in voting if the voting right has been lent out.
3 Politicians *disclose their vested interests.*
4 Politicians who meet and communicate professionally with stakeholders must have these meetings recorded by state television. These meetings are broadcast on state television and stored on the intranet.
5 Violations result in imprisonment for politicians and lobbyists. Politicians are also occupationally banned.

§66 **Prohibition of corruption**[122]

1 Politicians who act outside the requirements of the law applicable to them or are remunerated outside their state remuneration are liable to prosecution.
2 The affected population decides on the remuneration of politicians in the annual budget vote.

§67[123] **Immunity**[124]

1 Politicians *cannot be held legally responsible for their statements in state* and political *bodies.*
2 *The law may provide for other types of immunity and extend them to additional persons.*
3 Immunity remains limited to statements. Actions must comply with the applicable laws, including those of politicians.
4 Politicians are subject to official liability in their state activities.

---

120 BV Art.161
121 Ministry of State Organisation - 8.6.4.4 Delegates, 9.10.10 Lobbyists in the legislative process
122 Ministry of State Organisation - 12.1 Corruption and crime in the state system
123 BV Art.162
124 Ministry of State Organisation - 12.2 Immunity, 12.5 Punitive measures for politicians

5 Politicians are controlled by the citizens and sanctioned if necessary. Sanctions result in a committee of enquiry, new elections and, if there are violations of the law in office, also civil and criminal law court proceedings.

§68 Popular empowerment[125]

1 The people shall at all times have the right to authorise themselves to be subject to the control of any ministry. This requires a majority vote in favour of the empowerment quorum.

2 Ministry staff, politicians, candidates and their programmes are bound by the will of the people. If all those responsible for a ministry disregard the will of the people, those citizens entitled to vote take control of the ministry.

3 The Ministry of State Organisation shall be responsible for the proper democratic implementation of the popular empowerment procedure and shall convene a committee for this purpose.

4 It shall provide for the provisional management of the ministry and shall be bound by the instructions of the committee. No new laws may be enacted for this remit during this period. The committee ensures the immediate removal from office of individual employees of the ministry, of an entire ministry or of several ministries. If elected politicians are removed from office, a new election is immediately held for the affected posts.

5 If the Ministry of State Organisation itself is affected, the Federal Moderator's Office takes over the moderation of all necessary procedures. The staff of an affected ministry is replaced by citizens from disaster management, who remain in office until the following politicians are elected to recruit new staff.

6 Employees removed from office by popular empowerment are banned for life from all political parties and given occupational bans from state service.

7 New staff are recruited from the ministry's respective party.

---

125 Ministry of State Organisation - 12.3 Popular empowerment

Title 3: State powers

Chapter 1: Control of Power

§69[126] Separation of powers[127]

1 The organisation of the authorities shall be based on the principle of separation of powers. No agency may exercise state power in an uncontrolled and unlimited manner.
2 Those who perform state functions *are bound by the constitution*, laws and the will of affected citizens.
4 The four powers are the executive, the legislative, the judicial and the mediative. All four powers are controlled by the people through direct elections, committees, quorums and voting.
a. The executive is exercised by the employees of all ministries, to whom ministers and deputy ministers are superior as directly elected politicians.
b. Legislation is exercised by ministers, affected citizens or the people.
c. The judiciary is exercised by the Ministry of Justice with directly elected judges.
d. The mediative is exercised by the ministries of state organisation, digital affairs and media with directly elected federal moderators, administrators and directors.

§70[128] Superintendence[129]

1 The parties and citizens shall exercise supreme *supervision over* the ministries, their administration, *the courts and the other agencies of the* state.
2 *The* supervisory bodies *provided for in the law may not be subject to any confidentiality obligations.* These are namely the

---

126KV Art.66
127Ministry of State Organisation - 7 Separation of powers
128BV Art.169
129Ministry of State Organisation - 12.1 Corruption and Crime in the State System, Ministry of Labour - 20.2 Audit of State Agencies, Ministry of Media - 12 Surveillance Television, Ministry of Digital Affairs - 6 Statistical Office, 15.4 People-Controlled Politician, Ministry of Security - 7 Police, 2.1.2.1 Audit Services, Ministry of Justice - 5.6.3 Public Prosecutor's Office

monitoring teams of Surveillance Television, investigating officers of the police, public prosecutors and the Company Auditing Agency.

3 Citizens exercise oversight by observing or receiving state services and auditing them at the same time. If they find misconduct, they have the right to report the matter to the police, the Public Prosecutor's Office or the Federal Moderator's Office, or to take direct management of politicians via the intranet.

§71[130] Review of effectiveness[131]

1 By means of a quorum, citizens ensure *that the measures of the* state *are checked for their effectiveness* and correspond to the will of the people. Measures taken by the state can be changed or stopped by a repeal quorum. Ongoing measures of the state initiated by politicians can be stopped by the deselection quorum or the veto quorum.

2 The Ministry of Digital Affairs regularly compiles all state data into future forecasts through algorithms.

3 The Ministry of Media Affairs, through Party Television in co-production with the ministries, portrays the day-to-day work of the ministries.

4 The ministries of security, justice, labour, media and digital jointly set up monitoring teams. Through Surveillance Television, unannounced searches of a monitoring team in the ministries are filmed and published or undercover investigators with hidden cameras are infiltrated.

---

130 BV Art.170

131 Ministry of State Organisation - 12.1 Corruption and crime in the state system, Ministry of Labour - 20.2 Audit of state agencies, 20.4 Accountability, Ministry of Media - 12 Surveillance Television, 10 Party Television, Ministry of Digital Affairs - 6 Statistical Office, 2.1.2.1 Digital Service, 15.3 Algoracle, Ministry of Security - 7 Police, 2.1.2.1 Audit services, Ministry of Justice - 5.6.3 Public Prosecutor's Office

§72[132] Right of initiative and right of motion[133]

1 All ministers have *the right (...) to take initiatives* and implement them directly.

2 All deputy ministers shall have *the right to submit suggestions as motions*, to have them negotiated by the Council of Ministers and *to submit them* as *initiatives to* the ministers.

3 All Party members shall have the right to submit suggestions as motions, to have them negotiated by the Party Council and to submit them as initiatives to the ministers.

4 All citizens have the right to formulate suggestions as initiatives, with which they open an initiative quorum. If the quorum is triggered, the initiative is negotiated and voted on in a committee.

5 All citizens have the right to submit suggestions as petitions to the Federal Moderator's Office, to have them published on the intranet and to have them rated by users. After expiry of the petition deadline of 2 weeks, the petition text is submitted to the ministers as a suggestion. Citizens are entitled to a response within 6 months.

6 The filming of an initiative on which the people are to vote is obligatory. The Ministry of Media Affairs ensures production, broadcasting and archiving.

7 The Ministry of State Organisation shall decide *on the validity of initiatives that have been taken.*

8 The Ministry of State Organisation shall regulate the details by law and may create further opportunities for expressing the will of the people.

---

132 BV Art.160, 173
133 Ministry of State Organisation - 9.10.3 Right of Initiative, 9.10.11.7 Citizens' Initiative, Ministry of Media - 7 Government Television

§73 Implementation of initiatives[134]

1 An initiative adopted by a majority must be implemented by the government.
2 Ministers may implement their own or other initiatives directly if only their ministry is affected. Ministers are only entitled to make laws, regulations, administrative instructions and service instructions out of the initiatives.
3 If several ministries are affected, all participants must agree on the implementation. If this is not possible, either the citizens in a committee or the party council and the council of ministers of all ministries involved must negotiate and vote on it.
4 Initiatives by citizens brought forward by the initiative quorum are negotiated and voted on by citizens in a committee. Affected ministers have only an advisory function and must implement the decisions. Decisions can lead to constitutional articles, laws, regulations, municipal laws, administrative instructions or service instructions.
5 Initiatives by deputy ministers and party councillors can be implemented or rejected by ministers.
6 Before a law comes into force, a vote of the people or affected citizens must take place immediately or as part of the annual budget vote.

§74[135] Form of decrees[136]

1 The people shall *enact* the articles of the constitution of the country.
2 Ministers issue Law-making *regulations within the framework of* the country's constitution, namely laws and regulations.
3 Other elected politicians issue Law-making regulations, namely court decisions, municipal laws, statutes, administrative instructions or service instructions.
4 All Law-making provisions are included by the Ministry of Justice in the directory of laws as a new profile and provided

---

134 Ministry of State Organisation - 9.10.3 Right of initiative, 9.10.11.7 Citizens' initiative
135 BV Art.163
136 Ministry of State Organisation - 9.10.5 Law-making provisions

with links for quorums.

a. The veto quorum obtains the participation of citizens in the ongoing legislative process through a committee.

b. The repeal quorum obtains the abolition or modification of the relevant legislative provision by a committee.

c. The deselection quorum brings about the new election of the responsible politicians.

d. The revision quorum shall obtain the abolition or amendment of the relevant constitutional articles by a committee.

§75[137] Legislation[138]

1 All important Law-making provisions shall be enacted in the form of the law. *These include in particular the basic provisions on:*

a. the exercise of political rights;

b. the restrictions on constitutional rights;

c. the rights and duties of persons;

d. the group of persons liable to pay levies and the object and assessment of levies;

e. the tasks and services of the ministries;

f. the obligations of municipalities to assist in the implementation *and enforcement* of Law-making provisions;

g. the organisation and procedure of the authorities of all ministries.

2 The ministers give the laws for the ministry of their responsibility. Laws require *the consent* of the affected population and must *be revisable if requested by a majority of those entitled to vote.*

3 All laws enacted by ministers are considered provisional until the annual budget vote and come into force after a majority of over 60% in the voting.

4 Urgent or controversial laws may be negotiated and voted on at any time by the ministry or after a veto quorum in a committee.

5 The cooperation of several ministries is moderated by federal

---

137 BV Art.164, 51

138 Ministry of State Organisation - 9.7.6.2 Reconciliation of laws, 9.10 Legislation, 9.10.5 Law-making provisions

facilitators from the Ministry of State Organisation.

6 The date of repeal or revision of a law shall be determined by the repeal quorum of that law.

7 More detailed provisions on quorums shall be determined by the Ministry of State Organisation in the law.

§76[139] Legislation in case of urgency[140]

1 A law whose entry into *force cannot be delayed may be declared* urgent by a *majority of the members of* the responsible council *and may be brought into force immediately. It shall be limited in time.* The time limit ends at the latest with the annual budget vote on all enacted laws of the previous year. There, the population decides whether the law may remain in force.

2 *If, in respect of a law declared to* be urgent, a committee or a vote is demanded by those entitled to vote by veto quorum, *that* law shall *cease to have effect if it is not passed by committee* and vote.

3 A law *declared to* be urgent *which has no constitutional basis shall* not come into force until it has been adopted by a vote of the people by a majority of 75%. *It shall be limited in time.* The time limit ends at the latest with the conclusion of a constitutional committee at which it is decided whether a revision of the constitution will declare the law lawful or whether the law will be repealed.

4 *A law declared to* be urgent *which is not passed in the voting cannot be renewed.*

§77 Revision of the laws[141]

1 30% of those entitled to vote may trigger a veto quorum within a legislative process.

2 50% may trigger a repeal quorum at any time after the law is enacted.

3 After the quorum has been triggered, these requests shall be

---

139 BV Art.165
140 Ministry of State Organisation - 9.10.8 Urgent laws
141 Ministry of State Organisation - 9.5.14 Veto quorum, 9.5.15 Repeal quorum

negotiated in a committee and submitted to the people for voting.

§78[142] Publicity of meetings[143]

1 *The meetings of* all state bodies are *public.* They are broadcast on Government Television and on the intranet and can be accessed via the intranet for 100 years.
2 Ministers decide independently or citizens decide by veto quorum whether public meetings should also become interactive to involve citizens.

§79 Venues[144]

1 The venues for policy-making are basically the buildings of the ministries, their council buildings and party headquarters, as well as public squares and the intranet.
2 The digital intranet-based and real presence are placed on an equal footing. The ministries of media and digital affairs shall ensure multimedia implementation through appropriate means.
3 Those entitled to vote may raise their votes anywhere in the country through quorums and may cast their votes in committees and ballots.
4 Final votes on persons, laws or constitutional articles can only be cast at polling stations in every town hall in the country. Voting is possible at voting computers there for one week.
5 Committees shall be held in public places. Free admission must not be restricted. In case of large crowds, suitable venues must be found for follow-up meetings. Reference to digital participation is permissible in the event of increased costs so as not to exceed the approved budget.
6 Committees are held in different locations with a favourable

---

142BV Art.158
143Ministry of State Organisation - 9.4 Real and Digital Events, 9.4.1 Transmission
144Ministry of State Organisation - 8.6.2 Council of Ministers, 8.6.4 Party Council, 9.4 Real and Digital Events, 9.6.5 Venues

attitude and an unfavourable attitude on the part of the local resident population.

§80 Capacity to negotiate and quorum[145]

1 Ministers decide autonomously in accordance with the will of the people. A new veto quorum is opened for each decision-making process, a repeal quorum for each law-making decision.
a. If 30% of those entitled to vote reject a decision by the veto quorum, the decision is negotiated in a committee.
b. In representative democracy, if 40% of the members of the Council of Ministers reject a decision of their minister, the decision is negotiated in the Council of Ministers.
2 Ministers must convene a committee for the following deciders:
a. in the case of urgent laws that are to come into force immediately and not after the next annual budget vote.
b. for new one-off or recurring cash payments that were not part of the past budget vote.
3 Ministries have a quorum if the ministers are present in real or digital form.
4 Councils of Ministers constitute a quorum if all deputy ministers are present in real or digital form at the same time.
5 Party councils are quorate if all delegated party members are present in person or digitally at the same time.
6 Committees shall constitute a quorum if 20% of those entitled to vote are present in person or digitally.
7 Digital participation requires motions to be submitted before the real meeting and digital voting to take place at the same time as the real voting.

---

145 Ministry of State Organisation - 9.7 Voting, 9.7.3 Majorities

§81[146] Required majorities[147]

1 Templates put to a *vote of the people,* the citizens of individual municipalities or the members of the councils *are adopted if* at least 30% of those entitled to vote take part in the voting and a *majority* of 65% support the decision.

2 The percentage requirements for majority ratios leading to the adoption or rejection of a template can be changed by the majority quorum. As soon as 65% of a voting decide in favour of other majority ratios, the newly determined majority ratios shall be applied when counting the votes.

3 The result of a municipality's voting shall be deemed to be its valid municipal practice, provided that the municipality administers itself through a subsidiarity vote in the affected ministry.

§82 State of exception[148]

1 If there is no legal basis for a state of affairs and there is imminent danger, a state of exception can be declared. Ministers are authorised to declare a state of lawlessness and report it to the Ministry of State Organisation. The Minister of State Organisation and the mayor shall declare a state of exception.

2 All laws enacted in a state of exception are considered urgent laws. The citizens affected vote on them within a maximum of 3 weeks.

3 The Council of Exception is composed of all 18 ministers for laws that must be enacted immediately.

4 Laws that must be in force within 7 days are enacted by the ministers and the responsible council by way of representative legislation.

5 The Ministry of State Organisation shall regulate the details in the law.

146BV Art.142
147Ministry of State Organisation - 9.7.3 Majorities
148Ministry of State Organisation - 12.6 State of exception

§83 Flexible democracy[149]

1 The people of the nation and the affected citizens of the municipalities decide whether they want to be directly, indirectly or representatively involved in ministerial decision-making and legislation.
2 This decision can be made for individual ministries and on a municipal or national level.
3 70% of those entitled to vote must vote in a quorum to cede votes to responsible councillors in order to introduce representative democracy.
4 20% of those eligible to vote must vote in a quorum for direct citizen participation in order to introduce direct democracy.
5 Those entitled to vote may lend out their voting rights to delegates or party wing leaders of the parties at any time and retrieve them at any time. Those entitled to vote may decide for each of the parties individually whether to lend out their voting rights.
6 In the case of representative democracy, ministers must vote on laws and regulations with the responsible council. They need a 65 per cent majority of all MPs for this.
7 The council of each ministry is assisted by all state departments in an advisory capacity, as is the case with direct participation in the committees.
8 The political processes adapt flexibly to the dynamic willingness of citizens to participate in each individual case. Citizens can directly, indirectly or representatively determine the decision-making of one or more ministries or issues.

Section 1: Direct democracy

§84 Political civil rights[150]

1 Political voting rights within the scope of all ministries are available to all domestic nationals who have reached the age of 18.

---

149 Ministry of State Organisation - 9.1 Dynamic Democracy
150 Ministry of Media Affairs - 5.7 Interactivity, Ministry of Digital Affairs - 11.3 Admission, Ministry of Finance - 9 State expenditure, Ministry of Justice - 7.5.1 Restriction of rights, Ministry of State

2 Domestic nationals who have reached the age of 10 are entitled to political voting rights to the extent of the ministries of education and family.

3 Those entitled to vote may participate in the elections, voting, committees, polls and quorums of the International Union in which the inland is located, the nation and the municipality in which they live. They may take popular initiatives in international affairs and popular initiatives in national affairs and citizens' initiatives in municipal affairs and sign petitions.

4 All domestic citizens have the right to participate directly in domestic governance, for which the ministries of media, digital affairs, finance and state organisation are primarily responsible.

5 Nationals who are required to live under a law may vote on it.

6 Domestic nationals who are affected by a politician's policy are allowed to vote on him or her.

7 Citizens can delegate further tasks and powers to the ministries.

8 Domestic nationals who have been legally sentenced to imprisonment have only limited political rights for the duration of their imprisonment. The Ministry of Justice determines the details in the law.

§85 Quorum[151]

1 By means of a quorum, those entitled to vote can cast their vote in order to achieve a quorum from a fixed number. Those entitled to vote are thereby entitled to submit a direct-democratic decision on a state norm or office to all those entitled to vote.

2 There is no time limit on voting for a quorum. As soon as the specified number of votes is reached, a committee or a vote is triggered.

3 Various quorums may be instituted to express the will of those entitled to vote. These are at least the:

---

a. Quorum quorum whereby quorums are established or abolished;
b. Deselection quorum, it determines when the office of a politician is re-elected.
c. Repeal quorum, it determines when a norm becomes invalid or amended.
d. Veto quorum, which determines when citizens must be involved in state decision-making processes.
e. Revision quorum, which determines when the constitution is amended.
f. Majority quorum, which determines whether the affected majority ratios, which are the threshold for voting, are negotiated and changed.
4 Further quorums shall be determined by the Ministry of State Organisation in the law.
5 The majority ratios applicable to a quorum may be additionally indicated by those entitled to vote by percentage when casting their vote. The valid majority ratios for the next triggering of this quorum result from the median of all indicated percentages.

§86 Voting[152]

1 Voting is the only legitimate decider of all state action.
2 The citizens execute them within their municipality. The people perform them throughout the country. The peoples execute them in their countries. Citizens are entitled to vote if they are affected by a condition and belong to the municipality, nation or nations affected.
3 Voting takes place,
a. when ministers request it,
b. after the triggering of a quorum,
c. at the end of committees,
d. in the course of the annual budget vote.
4 Voting may be offered to voters as a package, but it must always be possible to vote individually.

---

152 Ministry of State Organisation - 9.7 Voting

§87[153] Mandatory referendum[154]

1 The people *and affected citizens* abroad shall be submitted to a vote:

a. *accession to collective security organisations, (...) supranational communities* or an International Union, and therein the change between two stages of integration;

b. international treaties, which may be bilateral, multilateral or under international law;

c. Changes to the territory of the nation.

2 *The following shall be submitted to the people for voting:*

a. *Amendments* to *the* constitution;

b. Popular *initiatives for a total revision of the* constitution;

c. Popular *initiatives for partial revision of the* Constitution;

d. *Changes in the* territory of all municipalities, *except for boundary corrections* between municipalities.

e. inter-municipal *treaties that are incompatible with the constitution;*

f. the annual budget vote for the state budget of the coming year;

g. the annual voting on all laws enacted during the previous year;

h. the quarterly voting in the event of war on whether and when to sign a surrender or continue to wage war;

i. whether international treaties should be negotiated either by the responsible ministers or by a committee;

j. *the* laws *declared* urgent *which have no constitutional basis.* They must *be* put to *the* vote immediately;

k. the sale or other privatisation of state property;

l. policy decisions or initiatives designated for mandatory voting by a quorum or committee.

§88 Election weeks[155]

1 All voting on politicians, laws and constitutional articles is held over the course of a week.

---

153 BV Art.140, KV Art.61

154 Ministry of State Organisation - 9.7.5 Binding coordination topics, 9.10.8 Urgent laws

155 Ministry of State Organisation - 8.2.1.1 Election Week

2 All those entitled to vote may cast their vote at any town hall in the country during the week of the election.

3 The last voting day of an election week shall be a Sunday. The voting results shall be announced on the last election day. A prior announcement is inadmissible.

4 No more than 5 election weeks may be held in any 52-week period.

5 Within an election week, a maximum of 5 deciders may be voted on at the same time. The only exception is the budget vote, which takes place once a year.

§89[156] Citizens' initiatives[157]

1 Citizens' initiatives are drafts or templates that have been formulated. Drafts must first be negotiated by a committee to become a template. Templates are put directly to a vote. _In the case of_ drafts, _the_ minister makes the final decision on the _legal form in which the template is to be drafted._

2 Within the framework of the voting of an initiative, counter-drafts may be prepared which shall also be put to the vote.

3 An initiative may request that:

a. Enactment of a new article or articles _of the constitution;_

b. _Enactment of_ a new law or _a package of laws;_

c. Termination _or commencement of negotiations for the conclusion of a_ new inter-municipal _or international_ treaty;

d. Drafting of any other new government decision to be put to a vote;

e. Reallocation of competences between ministries;

f. Opening of a new ministry or closure of an existing ministry.

4 An initiative must always refer to innovations. Existing state conditions can be repealed or changed by means of quorums. Suggestions can be made via petitions.

5 Citizens can create initiatives themselves in the quorum directory in order to open an initiative quorum. If their initiative is declared invalid by the responsible ministry after a processing period of maximum 2 weeks, they have the right to have the responsible party check and correct the deficiencies.

---

156 KV Art.58, 59
157 Ministry of State Organisation - 9.10.11.7 Citizens' Initiative

6 Initiatives with an ongoing initiative quorum are eligible for 2 weeks of campaigning by the affected party.

7 An initiative has come into being if 10% of those entitled to vote support the request by joining the initiative quorum.

8 As soon as the required number of 10% of those entitled to vote is reached, the draft is negotiated in a committee and the template is put to a vote of the people or affected citizens. If a majority of 60% or more votes in favour of the template, it becomes a legal act.

9 The Ministry of State Organisation shall regulate the details in the law.

§90[158] Invalid initiatives[159]

1 The Ministry of Digital Affairs shall judge the validity by the votes collected in the initiative quorum. The affected ministry or ministries check the validity of initiatives.

2 Initiatives shall be declared invalid in whole or in part if they:
a. violate superior law for which no repeal quorum has yet reached the necessary votes to trigger the initiative quorum;
b. are demonstrably *impracticable.*

3 Initiatives declared invalid shall be left in the initiative quorum. Once the quorum is triggered, invalidated initiatives must also be negotiated and voted on in a committee, whether it is a draft or a template.

§91[160] Procedure for initiative and counter-draft[161]

1 A counter-draft can come from politicians and citizens. Citizens must get 0.005% of those entitled to vote to sign a petition for their initiative within 2 weeks.

2 Those entitled to vote shall vote *simultaneously on the initiative and the counter-draft* or counter-drafts.

---

158 KV Art.59
159 Ministry of State Organisation - 9.10.11.7.1 Invalidity of citizens' initiatives
160 BV Art.139b
161 Ministry of State Organisation - 9.10.11.6 Petition, 9.10.11.7.3 Counter-proposals for citizens' initiatives

3 You can vote for more than one template. If the two leading templates are only 5% apart, a run-off vote must be held. *In the run-off* vote, those entitled to vote *can indicate which* of the two leading templates *they give priority to.*

§92[162] Committees[163]

1 In accordance with the Constitution, citizens participate directly and democratically in the decision-making of the ministries, in particular in the making of law and the election of persons, through committees.
2 Committees are public interactive decision-making meetings between politicians, scientists, affected people, party wing representatives and citizens.
3 Committees may select and consult experts and affected persons for advice.
4 In committees, politicians negotiate with the people or affected citizens. There they:
a. Prepare elections of persons by formulating programmes and nominating candidates;
b. Existing norms reworded or new norms formulated and put to a vote;
c. Conflicts over responsibilities decided *between the highest* authorities;
d. *Pardons* issued.

§93 Convening of committees[164]

1 Committees can be convened by politicians and, by quorum, by affected citizens.
2 The ministries inform citizens in a timely and comprehensive manner about their plans.
3 They seek the views of citizens whose interests are affected.
4 Ministers are entitled to convene committees at any time.
5 Ministers shall convene a committee at least for the preparation of important decrees and other projects of

---

162 BV Art.157
163 Ministry of State Organisation - 9.6 Committee
164 Ministry of State Organisation - 9.6.3.2 Convocation

major significance as well as for important treaties under international law.

6 Committees give ministers the opportunity to spare their deselection quorum if there is strong opposition to a proposal. Committees can also damage the deselection quorum if they are convened too frequently.

7 Citizens can convene committees as soon as a quorum is reached.

§94 Digital participation in committees[165]

1 Committees shall be multi-media in order to involve all those entitled to vote in the negotiation process.

2 Committees are broadcast through the ministries of media and digital so that all those entitled to vote who are inland can participate in the committee in real or digital form.

3 The Ministry of Media Affairs provides media coverage of the proceedings and broadcasts them in real time on Government Television.

4 Participation allows those entitled to vote to influence decision-making via the intranet through surveys, suggestions and voting.

5 The Ministry of Digital Affairs shall ensure digital processing of the proceedings and enable those entitled to vote within the country to vote or contribute remotely.

6 The Ministry of State Organisation provides for three federal facilitators per committee:

a. Moderator for the panel, moderating ministers, politicians, affected citizens and scientists;

b. Moderator for the audience, moderates participating citizens in the venue;

c. Moderator for viewers moderates those entitled to vote at transmitting and receiving devices.

---

165 Ministry of State Organisation - 9.6.3.7 Media implementation, Ministry of Digital Affairs - 11 Intranet, 15.5 Policy Manager, Ministry of Media Affairs - 7.2.3.1 Election of persons committees, 7.2.3.5 Solution Finder (Legislation Committee), 7.2.3.5.4 Moderators, 7.2.3.5.5 Participation for viewers

§95 Committees in the election of persons process[166]

1 In the election of persons process, two different types of committees are held after the pre-election and before the run-off election.

2 After the pre-election, programmes and programme items that received majorities in the pre-election are combined in up to three programmes on the programme committee. Programme items that are similar are combined in one programme. Programme items that contradict each other are listed in different programmes.

3 Prior to the run-off election, candidates who must be members of the affected party shall be tested on the candidate committee as to their attitude and suitability for one of the three programmes from the programme committee.

4 In the election of persons process, the committees shall provide the wording of the programmes to be put to the run-off election and the two candidates running against each other for one programme each.

§96 Committees in the legislative process[167]

1 Committees are established in the direct route of legislation. Legislative proposals are formulated there and put to a vote.

2 The direct legislative route is taken when:

a. Ministers do so voluntarily,

b. the responsible council decides it with a majority of 65%,

c. the citizens demand it in a veto quorum or repeal quorum.

3 At the end of a committee, a majority formulation for a legal act should be available, which is voted on by all affected citizens.

4 In the same committee procedure that the ministries deal with the citizens, the nation deals with the municipalities and the parties with their party wings when it comes to formulating a policy. Those entitled to vote change, but the procedure remains the same. Either they are citizens or politicians of the

---

166 Ministry of State Organisation - 9.6.2.2 Committees in the election of persons process
167 Ministry of State Organisation - 9.6.2.1 Committees in the legislative process

affected international, national or municipal level, or they are party members.

§97[168] Committee of enquiry[169]

1 Committees of enquiry shall be convened as soon as an unlawful act is alleged to have been accompanied or abetted by state agencies.
2 In order to *fulfil* its *duties,* the committee of enquiry shall have the right to *information, the right of inspection and the power of investigation. Their scope shall be regulated by the Ministry of Justice* in the law.
3 The participants of the Investigation Committee guarantee truthful statements, fair procedures, professional knowledge and technical equipment.
4 Committees of enquiry are held during Surveillance Television shows, with the responsible Surveillance Television monitoring teams.

Section 2: Indirect democracy

§98[170] Ministers[171]

1 Ministers shall exercise *supreme authority* in their ministry, subject to *the rights of the people and* affected citizens.
2 Ministers have municipal elected deputies in each municipality.
a. The municipality may have municipal ministers without deputies after a successful subsidiarity vote.
b. The International Union may, after a successful subsidiarity vote, have international ministers in place of national ministers whose deputies are the municipal elected deputy ministers

---

168 BV Art.153
169 Ministry of State Organisation - 12.5.2 Committee of enquiry, Ministry of Justice - 5.4.5.2 Committee of enquiry, Ministry of Media Affairs - 12.3.4.1 Committee of enquiry
170 BV Art.148
171 Ministry of State Organisation - 8.3.1 Ministers, 8.3.2 Deputy ministers, 9.10.11.1 Indirect legislation

from the municipalities or the municipal ministers.

3 ministers and their deputies form the indirect route of legislation:

a. Ministers have the right to put proposed legislation directly to a referendum.

b. Deputy ministers have the right to put municipal by-law proposals directly to a citizens' vote.

c. International ministers have the right to put proposals for laws and international treaties directly to the affected peoples for a vote.

4 Ministers and senior officials are directly elected if they have Law-making or judicial powers in their office. Their term of office is linked to successful service in accordance with the will of the people. Those entitled to vote express this popular will in the deselection quorum, the fulfilment of which results in a new election.

§99 Ministries[172]

1 Ministries are the executive organs of the state. Their Law-making and jurisprudence activities are managed or supervised by the people or affected citizens through participation opportunities and quorums.

2 Ministries are divided into the 18 policy remits of the state. These are namely the ministries of labour, foreigners, education, digital affairs, family, finance, health, infrastructure, innovation, integration, justice, media, security, state organisation as well as Barter Economy, Planned Economy, Social Market Economy and Free Market Economy.

3 Each ministry has a party with any number of different party wings in order to be able to offer the affected population different solutions.

4 Each ministry is located in its own capital city. The council building and the party headquarters for that ministry are located there. The field offices of a ministry are located in the town halls of all municipalities.

---

172 Ministry of State Organisation - 4.1.2 Establishment and closure of ministries, 8.4 Ministries, 8.4.1 Capital city and field offices, 8.4.2 Create new ministry

5 Only the people can establish a new ministry or abolish an old one. If the people vote in favour, the constitution must be amended.

6 The duties and responsibilities of a new ministry must be fully described in the template before the people convene a new ministry in a voting.

7 The Ministry of State Organisation may, in voting with citizens and ministers, close an existing ministry or shift responsibilities between ministries.

§100 Party Council[173]

1 All citizens entitled to vote may select one delegate or one delegate per ministry.

2 Citizens entitled to vote have the choice to lend out their vote to a party member or party wing leader, So-called delegates.

3 The delegates shall form the Party Council.

4 The Party Council may request opinions from all employees of the ministry and vote in elections of persons and legislative processes.

5 Party councils meet in public in the council building of the respective capital city of the ministry and digitally on the intranet site of the party council.

6 Party councillors report and justify their decision on their voting behaviour to those citizens entitled to vote.

7 The municipal party council assumes the functions of the council of ministers in representative municipal policy if at least 90% of the citizens of the municipality have lent out their vote to delegates from their municipality and, after an appropriate quorum, a majority vote in favour.

8 Municipal exceptions are regulated by the Ministry of State Organisation in the law.

9 The party council shall be chaired by a federal moderator.

---

173 Ministry of State Organisation - 8.6.4 Party Council, 8.6.4.4 Delegates, 9.10.11.2 Indirect Voting

§101 Council of Ministers[174]

1 The Council of Ministers consists of all municipal directly elected deputy ministers and the respective minister.
2 As soon as the number of those entitled to vote in the deselection quorum has been reached, which led to the election victory, a new election of the respective member of the Council of Ministers shall take place.
3 Each municipality shall form a constituency and shall have one seat.
4 The meeting for the Council of Ministers takes place digitally on its intranet site and in real terms in the Council building in the capital city. The digital presence is equal to the real one.
5 The Council of Ministers ensures that all municipalities are equally well supported by the ministry. Good provision is based on the local needs of the municipality and does not have to be the same everywhere.
6 The deputy ministers represent a ministry in the municipal town hall and occupy an office there.
7 The Council of Ministers shall acquire or lose the representative responsibility as soon as the relevant quorum has been fulfilled or the Minister causes it to do so.
8 Through representative responsibility, the national or international procedures for elections of persons and legislation may be delegated to the Council of Ministers. In this regard, those entitled to vote are as follows:
a. Those entitled to vote in the election of persons process for ministers and senior officials of the ministry are the deputies. They shall exercise their voting rights in the committees and voting.
b. Those entitled to vote in the legislative process are the deputy ministers and the minister. They may submit, negotiate and vote on initiatives and counter-templates.
9 Municipal exceptions are regulated by the Ministry of State Organisation in the law.
10 The Council of Ministers is chaired by a federal facilitator.

174Ministry of State Organisation - 8.6.2 Council of Ministers

§102 International Council[175]

1 The International Council shall meet when at least two States are communitarised in at least one ministry.
2 It shall be responsible for international treaty negotiation, election of persons and legislative procedures if the peoples affected so declare in accordance with a participation quorum or veto quorum.
3 For treaty negotiation and legislation, those entitled to vote are deputy ministers, municipal ministers and international ministers. For the election of persons, those entitled to vote are deputy ministers and municipal ministers.
4 The other functions and procedures of the International Council shall be the same as those of the Council of Ministers.
5 Once all 18 ministries are administered internationally with another country, the transition to a new larger nation with national and municipal political levels takes place. The deputy ministers remain and form the Council of Ministers in larger number of municipalities. The international council is dissolved by the larger council of ministers. International ministers automatically become the new national ministers. The Ministry of Foreign Affairs determines the details in the law.

Chapter 3: Executive - Execution of law

§103[176] Government policy[177]

1 Ministers determine the goals *and means* of *government policy* in their ministry. They plan and coordinate state *activities in cooperation with* their staff as long as citizens do not lodge an appeal through a quorum.
2 They shall inform *the public about* their *activities in a timely and comprehensive manner.* For all citizens, all data on the intranet must be accessible without delay, at any time and

---

175 Ministry of State Organisation - 8.6.3 International Council, Ministry of Foreign Affairs - 5.8.2.2 Middle Ring, 5.8.2.3 Inner Ring
176 BV Art.180
177 Ministry of State Organisation - 9.8 Governments of the State, 9.8.3 Control

permanently for an unlimited period of time, and must be capable of being commented on and evaluated.

§104 Government decisions[178]

1 Each government forms itself for a project and makes its deciders for this individual case.
2 The government makes decisions in up to three democratic ways:
a. Indirectly, through directly elected ministers deciding.
b. Direct, through citizens deciding in committees and voting.
c. Representative, in that deputy, municipal, national or international ministers decide together with the party council, council of ministers or international council.
3 Any government decision from a. or c. may be negotiated by a veto quorum while the decision is still being made or by a repeal quorum after it has been passed in a committee.
4 In voting after a veto quorum or a participation quorum, a direct, indirect or representative way can be determined by citizens for further government decisions in the respective individual case or permanently.
5 Government decisions are namely laws, ordinances, municipal laws, statutes, administrative instructions or service instructions, except constitutional articles and court decisions.
6 Citizens decide as a people when government decisions affect the whole country. They decide as affected citizens when government decisions affect only that group of people, a municipality, a group of municipalities or several municipalities. They decide as peoples when government decisions affect several nations.

178 Ministry of State Organisation - 9.5.11 Participation quorum, 9.8 State governments, 9.8.1 Government decisions, 9.10.5 Law-making provisions, 9.10.11.3 Direct legislation, Direct voting, 9.10.11.9 Representative legislation, 9.10.11.10 Representative voting

§105 Liability for government decisions[179]

1 All ministers and politicians involved are liable for government decisions with their deselection quorum.

2 In the case of government decisions that contravene the oath of office to act for the good of the people, responsible ministers and politicians are personally liable under civil and criminal law. The Ministry of Justice shall determine further details in the law.[180]

3 Those entitled to vote may negotiate and vote on any government decision in a committee. Immediately after voting, those entitled to vote are jointly liable as nations, a nation or a municipality, depending on whether a government decision affects several countries, the whole country or only a local or limited part.

§106 Responsibility for government and control[181]

1 The people are responsible for the wording of the constitution and control whether it is observed by governments and ministries.

2 Citizens constitute the staff of party members who can stand for election to a politician's office with responsibility for government. Citizens are responsible for the selection of elected politicians and for their new election.

3 Citizens directly elect ministers for all 18 ministries, thereby empowering them to govern the ministry in question.

4 Citizens can also lend out their vote for the election of persons to party members or party wings, or give it to councillors and get it back by voting after a veto quorum.

5 Ministers have three paths open to them in their governance:

1) They make government decisions independently and rely on the silent consent of those entitled to vote.

2) They involve those entitled to vote in the government

---

179 Ministry of State Organisation - 9.8.4 Liability

180 Ministry of Justice - 8.14.2 Abuse of office, 8.14.5 State protection criminal law

181 Ministry of State Organisation - 9.8.2 Responsibility, 9.8.3 Control, 9.8.4 Liability, 9.9.5.2 Indirect election of persons, 9.10.11.1 Indirect legislation

decision through a committee and get an immediate vote for that individual case. This way is prescribed for controversial government decisions and those that deviate from the election programme that led to the election victory of involved ministers, or if more money is to be spent than was approved in the budget vote.

3) Ministers negotiate publicly on Government Television with the responsible council and vote together in an open ballot.

6 Citizens participate in committees and determine the wording of government decisions in them if

a. Ministers to convene a committee.

b. Citizens can convene a committee by veto quorum.

7 Citizens can control the indirect 1) and representative 3) forms of government through:

a. Voting for the veto quorum that convenes a committee while the governmental process is still underway.

b. Voting for the repeal quorum, which convenes a committee to negotiate, amend or repeal past government decisions.

c. Vote for the deselection quorum to bring about new elections for affected politicians. Those entitled to vote have one vote per term to bring about a new election for the affected office.

d. Refusal to approve the annual discharge of ministers or the budget item in the coming year. Government decisions are thereby rendered ineffective or renegotiated.

8 Citizens elect 18 deputy ministers at the municipal level who are responsible for the local implementation of government decisions.

9 Government decisions without an immediate vote are considered provisional until the annual budget vote of the following year and the approval of all ministers therein. The proviso is that government decisions can be reversed without any right to compensation. Exceptions to this are government decisions with an immediate vote.

§107[182] **Powers of the governments**[183]

1 Governments have *the following duties and powers:*
a. Ministers and their deputies shall supervise the administration and other agencies of their ministry.
b. The Ministry of Media Affairs shall report regularly to the citizens on the management of all ministries and on the state of the country and of all countries that are in the same International Union.
c. The Ministry of State Organisation, in cooperation with the Ministries of Media and Digital Affairs, conducts the elections and voting of citizens.
d. Federal facilitators shall handle complaints to the extent provided by law.
2 The Ministry of State Organisation may delegate *further duties and powers to governments* in the law.
3 If no agreement is reached between the ministers, a committee shall be convened by the Ministry of State Organisation.

§108[184] **Composition and election of the government**[185]

1 Each government shall meet in an appropriate number for each individual case. The number shall be determined by the ministries affected in an individual case.
2 The government consists of at least one and up to 18 directly elected ministers.
3 As a rule, there are 18 governments, one for each ministry. Ministers are alone in the government of their ministry.
4 Ministers or the citizens may involve other persons, politicians, ministries, councils or committees in the government.
5 The Ministry of State Organisation moderates cooperation as soon as several ministries are involved in a government decision. It checks reports to see if another ministry is involved. Reports can come from governing or presumably

---

182 BV Art.173
183 Ministry of State Organisation - 9.8.2 Responsibility, 9.8.3 Control
184 BV Art.175
185 Ministry of State Organisation - 4.2 Cooperation processes, 9.8.2.1 Ministers in government

affected ministers, or from citizens via a veto quorum.

6 Ministers are elected by those entitled to vote in an election of persons. There, government programmes and candidates for the leadership of the ministry compete against each other. Once the number of votes in the deselection quorum reaches the number of votes needed to win the past election, there are new elections for that position.

§109[186] Chair of the government[187]

1 The government decision of an individual ministry shall be chaired by the respective minister.

2 For two or more involved ministries, a Federal Moderator shall *chair the government.*

§110[188] Collegial principle[189]

1 The ministers decide unanimously *as colleagues if* several ministries are involved in a government decision.

2 Ministers and politicians decide according to the will of the people and the laws.

3 Ministers, together with their staff, implement the will of the people and the laws as a ministry.

4 *For the preparation and execution, the business* of the governments shall be *distributed among the* ministries *according to remits.*

5 *Business shall be delegated to the* ministries *or the administrative units under them for independent execution; in doing so, compliance with* the law must *be ensured.*

6 If something is decided in voting with someone, the voting right is the same for all participants involved. In the case of equal majority ratios, the circle of ministers involved is extended by the elected politicians involved. All participants involved must always be granted an equal number of those entitled to vote. The voting of non-elected staff members is secret. The circle of

---

186 BV Art.176
187 Ministry of State Organisation - 9.8.2.2 Cooperation between several ministries
188 BV Art.177
189 Ministry of State Organisation - 9.8.2.3 Collegial Principle

those entitled to vote can be increasingly extended to include the affected state employees, up to and including all affected citizens. If two ministers decide something in voting with each other, dissenting votes can be eliminated by concessions elsewhere. These negotiations are also always public to allow citizens a veto quorum.

7 Government negotiations are broadcast simultaneously on Government Television and published permanently on the intranet.

§111[190] Administration[191]

1 The ministers shall administer the administration of their ministry and ensure its expedient *organisation and the purposeful fulfilment of tasks.*

2 The state administration is *divided* into remits. Each department is administered by a ministry. *Each* ministry *is headed by* a minister. The deputy ministers administer the municipal administration. The international ministers administer the international administration.

3 All politicians have the authority to control the service of their ministry's authorities in accordance with the laws and norms.

4 The administrative tasks are digitised with the help of the ministries of media and digital and published for the citizens affected.

5 The Ministry of State Organisation is responsible for procedural matters and harmonisation projects.

6 International ministers for participating nations, ministers for the nation and deputy ministers for their municipality can:

a. establish establishments and other institutions under state and private law;

b. participate in institutions under *state and private law;*

c. transfer state *tasks to private parties and institutions outside the administration.*

7 The *law shall regulate in particular:*

---

190 BV Art.178, KV Art.95

191 Ministry of State Organisation - 4.1 State Procedure Law, 9.8.5 Administration

a. the basic features of the organisation and tasks of establishments and institutions set up by the State;
b. Nature and framework of the delegation *of legislative powers* below the *regulations;*
c. Type and scope of state participations;
d. Type and scope of the transfer of a state *task, insofar as this has as its object a (...) service or authorises the restriction of fundamental rights or the levying of charges.*
8 *These state agencies are under the supervision of the ministry* for which they work. Politically responsible are the responsible ministers or deputy ministers.

§112[192] Heterarchical organisational principle[193]

1 Ministers, through their ministries, shall ensure the execution of *legislation, decisions* of committees or councils *and judgments of judicial authorities of the Ministry of Justice.*
2 Ministers and their staff form a colleagues. Superior relationships do not apply when it comes to introducing new methods for implementing the will of the people.
3 All persons working for a ministry shall statistically evaluate their performance and make suggestions for improvement.
4 The staff members responsible for implementation shall at all times have a direct right of proposal for efficiency improvements to their minister.
5 For successful improvement proposals with a proven increase in efficiency through savings in the budget of the coming year, a one-off payment equivalent to 10% of the increase in efficiency in the first year is made.
6 All employees of a ministry have a right of co-determination through which the implementation of new requirements by citizens or the modification of existing work activities of the ministry must be negotiated with them. Ministers must hold these negotiations in public and have them broadcast by Government Television.
7 Due to the political responsibility through direct election, ministers retain the right of final decision.

---

192 BV Art.182
193 Ministry of State Organisation - 8.4.3 Internal heterarchy

8 If proposals from staff members are ignored by ministers, the staff members may report this to the Federal Moderator's Office. If a proposal is also ignored here, affected staff members may contact the independent media and publish the facts.

Chapter 4: Mediative - Mediation of law

§113 Media democracy[194]

1 In a democracy, the fourth power in the state alongside the legislature, the executive and the judiciary is the media. Mediation between the powers and the people is the responsibility of the ministries of state organisation, media and digital affairs.

2 State media transmit political information, enable communication between citizens and politicians, ensure transparent government work and opportunities for citizens to exercise control.

3 Four separate broadcasting organisations shall be created which shall

a. broadcast municipal, national, international and economic government negotiations of all kinds and allow interactive participation in committees. This broadcaster accompanies the legislation.

b. portray the work of the ministries unfree in the sense of these ministries. This broadcasting station accompanies the executive and the judiciary.

c. display the work of all state organs freely, covertly and unannounced and immediately punish discovered offences legally.

d. film or interactively translate any state-funded educational work and store it for public access.

4 Politicians and state bodies ensure that their contents are informative and entertaining, and that citizens can participate

---

194 Ministry of State Organisation - 4.4 Federal Moderator's Office, 7.1 Mediative, 7.1.1 State television, 7.1.1.2 Intranet, Ministry of Digital Affairs - 7 Digital data protection, 13 People's Innovation Company Intranet, Ministry of Media Affairs - 5 State broadcasting, 7.2 Programme, 10.1 Programme, 12.3 Programme, 13.2 Programme

in state decision-making in an interactive and multimedia way.

5 Party manifestos and laws are filmed, broadcast and stored for public access by state television before the final voting.

6 Committees are held as interactive talk shows, broadcast in real time via multimedia and stored for public access. Music, dance and song are fixed entertaining components to activate the audience during public policy events.

7 The intranet serves as a secure and democratically controlled communication line between citizens and the state.

8 The ministries of media and digital ensure that the population is equipped with up-to-date digital voting tools to participate interactively in political and state negotiations.

9 The Ministry of State Organisation ensures cooperation between ministries and between the state and its citizens through the Federal Moderator's Office.

§114[195] Federal Moderator's Office[196]

1 The Federal Moderator's Office *is the general staff unit* of governments and serves to moderate government negotiations between ministries, ministers and citizens.

2 It is considered an independent agency within the Ministry of State Organisation and employs moderators.

3 Moderators can be appointed for committees and government negotiations. It is their duty to conduct the negotiations in a neutral manner, giving equal validity to the interests of both the ministries and the citizens.

4 They are the point of contact for citizens who are not sure which procedure is appropriate to assert their interests. The Federal Moderator's Office maintains an *ombudsman's office for citizens*.

5 The Federal Moderator's Office decides *conflicts of jurisdiction between the highest authorities.*

---

195 BV Art.179, KV Art.96, BV Art.157
196 Ministry of State Organisation - 4.1 State Procedure Law, 4.4 Federal Moderator's Office, 4.4.1 Internal Service, 4.4.2 External Service

§115 Moderators[197]

1 Moderators are elected employees of the Ministry of State Organisation.
2 moderators have their own deselection quorum.
3 The Ministry of State Organisation maintains moderators for the national and municipal levels in the Federal Moderator's Office. The Ministry of Foreign Affairs is responsible for the international level.
4 moderators chair committees and meetings of the councils.
5 They appear on state television and the intranet to moderate negotiations and news.

Chapter 5: Judiciary - Jurisprudence

§116[198] Position of the National Court of Justice[199]

1 The National Court of Justice *is the supreme judicial agency of the* State.
2 The Ministry of Justice shall *determine the organisation and procedure* in the law.
3 The National Court of Justice administers *itself.* The leader is directly elected by the other judges of the National Court of Justice and receives a quorum for new election.
4 All judges of the National Court of Justice are directly elected by the people and receive a quorum for new election.

§117[200] Responsibilities of the National Court of Justice[201]

1 The *National Court of Justice shall have final* jurisdiction in disputes for infringement:
a. of national law;

---

197 Ministry of State Organisation - 4.4.3 Federal Moderators
198 BV Art.188
199 Ministry of Justice - 5.4.5 National Court of Justice
200 BV Art.189
201 Ministry of Justice - 5.4.5 National Court of Justice

b. of international law;

c. of inter-municipal law;

d. of municipal law;

e. of civil law or criminal law;

f. of national and municipal provisions on political *rights.*

2 It judges *disputes between the nation* and municipalities *or between* municipalities.

3 It shall judge revisions of court cases in the third instance.

4 *The law may establish further responsibilities of the National Court of* Justice.

5 *Acts of the committees* and the government *cannot be challenged in the National Court of* Justice, but through a quorum. *Exceptions are determined by the Ministry of Justice* in the law.

6 In the course of communitarisation by an International Union, responsibilities are transferred to an International Court of Justice.

§118[202] Admission to the National Court of Justice[203]

1 The law guarantees admission to the National Court of Justice.
2 For disputes that do not concern a legal question of fundamental importance, it *may provide for a limit on the amount in dispute.*
3 For (...) subject matters of the Constitution, *the law may exclude admission to the National Court of* Justice and refer it to the Constitutional Court.
4 The law may provide for a simplified procedure for manifestly unfounded appeals.

§119[204] Governing law[205]

The Constitution, the laws *and international law govern* the National Court of Justice *and the other authorities applying the law.*

---

202 BV Art.191
203 Ministry of Justice - 5.4.5 National Court of Justice
204 BV Art. 190
205 Ministry of Justice - 4.8 Areas of law

§120[206] Constitutional Court[207]

1 The Ministry of Justice provides a Constitutional Court.

2 The Constitutional Court is the first instance to judge *cases brought before it by a* constitutional complaint. The final instance in these constitutional proceedings is the Constitutional Committee.

3 The Constitutional Court shall be the court of last instance to hear cases referred to it by the National Court of Justice.

4 All judges of the Constitutional Court are directly elected by the people and receive a quorum for new election.

§121[208] Remit Courts[209]

1 The Ministry of Justice shall provide one Remit Court for each Ministry. The Ministry of Justice may *establish further responsibilities* of the Remit Courts in the law.

2 Remit Courts judge cases received from the Municipal Courts in second instance.

3 The Ministry of Justice may provide for *other judicial authorities in the law.*

4 All judges of the Remit Courts are directly elected by the people and receive a quorum for new election.

§122[210] Municipal Courts[211]

1 The Ministry of Justice shall provide a Municipal Court for each municipality for the adjudication *of civil,* criminal law or administrative *disputes in the* first instance.

2 Municipalities may *jointly establish* a Municipal Court as long as there is sufficient capacity.

3 All Municipal Court judges are directly elected by affected citizens of a municipality and receive a quorum for new election.

---

206 BV Art.191a
207 Ministry of Justice - 5.4.6 Constitutional Court
208 BV Art.191a
209 Ministry of Justice - 5.4.4 Remit Courts
210 BV Art.191b
211 Ministry of Justice - 5.4.3 Municipal Courts

§123[212] Courts[213]

<u>*1 The independence of the courts is guaranteed.*</u> The judges are directly elected.
<u>*2 Court hearings shall be public. The reasons for the judgements shall be given in writing. The law shall specify the exceptions.*</u>
<u>*3*</u> The Ministry of Justice regulates the responsibility <u>*of the courts*</u> in the law.

§124[214] Judicial independence[215]

In their jurisprudence, judges *are equally committed to the law* and to those entitled to vote.

§125 Judicial instances[216]

1 All disputes, except constitutional disputes, shall be heard at different instances if the plaintiff or defendant so requests within 12 months of the date of judgment.

2 The first instance shall be the Municipal Courts. If the plaintiff and the defendant are not located in the same catchment area of the Municipal Court, the plaintiff's place of jurisdiction shall be deemed responsible.

3 The second instance is the Remit Courts, which hear appeal cases.

4 The third instance is the National Court of Justice, which hears revision cases.

5 The fourth instance is the Constitutional Court, which tries unconstitutional laws.

6 Video calls between court locations in court hearings are permissible in order to reduce travel time and costs.

7 Constitutional complaints are accepted by the Municipal Courts and forwarded directly to the Constitutional Court. The Constitutional Court may call in judges from the relevant

---

212 KV Art.97
213 Ministry of Justice - 5.4 Courts
214 BV Art.191c
215 Ministry of Justice - 5.6.1 Judges
216 Ministry of Justice - 5 Court proceedings, 5.4.3 Municipal Courts, 5.4.4 Remit Courts, 5.4.5 National Court of Justice, 5.4.6 Constitutional Court

Remit Courts.

Title 4: Federalism

Chapter 1: Federal foundations

§126[217] Principles of federalism[218]

1 International Union, nation and municipalities *support each other in the fulfilment of their tasks.*
2 They work together in an entrepreneurially efficient and cooperative democratic manner.
3 *They owe one another consideration and assistance.*
4 *They shall provide each other with office and legal assistance.*
5 Municipalities are recipients of instructions from the nation as long as the people do not shift all or some of the responsibilities of a ministry in a subsidiarity vote.
6 A confederation of states of individual or several ministries is the nation's directive-giver if the peoples of all member states shift the responsibilities of a ministry in a subsidiarity vote.
7 *Disputes between municipalities or between municipalities* and the nation *are resolved through negotiation and mediation whenever possible.* If necessary, a committee is convened by the Ministry of State Organisation or affected citizens through a veto quorum.
8 Responsibility and authority can be transferred between the levels, by ministers with a motions or by citizens with a quorum, in a subsidiarity vote.

§127[219] Population and territory of municipalities[220]

1 The nation or nations shall protect or safeguard the existence *and territory of* municipalities.
2 *Changes in the population of the* municipalities require the consent *of the affected population* in the affected municipalities.

---

217 BV Art.44
218 Ministry of State Organisation - 11.2 Political levels
219 BV Art.53
220 Ministry of State Organisation - 11.5.1 Municipality

3 Changes of territory between municipalities require the consent *of the affected population and* municipalities and approval *by* a national committee.

4 Boundary adjustments can be made between municipalities *by treaty.* The affected population must agree to the treaties.

§128 Municipal self-determination[221]

1 Insofar as a ministry is administered municipally after a subsidiarity vote, the responsibility of national or international politicians of this ministry in the territory of this municipality shall cease.

2 The election of deputy ministers is now considered an election for municipal minister.

3 Ministries administered municipally have the right to make decisions independently of the national ministry. In return, the right of national influence ceases to exist.

4 The affected citizens of the municipality lose voting rights at the national level in this ministry.

5 The ministries of justice and security may not be administered municipally. However, the staff of these ministries implement municipal law, provided it does not violate the constitution.

§129[222] Autonomy of the municipalities[223]

1 The nation preserves *the autonomy of municipalities* by allowing citizens of a municipality to vote by absolute majority in a subsidiarity referendum to administer themselves in all matters relating to one or more ministries, as long as they remain faithful to the constitution.

2 It leaves *the* municipalities with their own *tasks*, which are determined by affected citizens with their deputy ministers.

3 It leaves *the* municipalities with sufficient sources of funding *and helps to ensure that they have the necessary financial resources to fulfil their tasks.*

---

221 Ministry of State Organisation - 11.5.2 Municipal level
222 BV Art.47
223 Ministry of State Organisation - 10.3 Subsidiarity voting, 11.5 Municipal policy

4 Municipalities are allowed to advertise for money to their constituents during the annual budget vote.
5 The ministries of security and justice cannot be administered municipally.

§130[224] Cultural protection areas and economic zones[225]

1 The autonomy of cultural protection areas *is guaranteed in accordance with* the municipal *right* to self-government.
2 The autonomy of the economic zones is guaranteed in accordance with the law of the ministries of Free Market Economy, Social Market Economy, Planned Economy and Barter Economy.
3 The nation shall *consider the potential impact on cultural protection areas* and economic zones in its actions.
4 In doing so, it takes into account *the* self-determined *situation of citizens* in these conurbations of subcultures.

Chapter 2: Federal Law

§131[226] Constitutional order[227]

1 The people shall protect *the constitutional order of the nation.* The nation protects the constitutional order of the municipalities. The nations protect the constitutional order of international ministries.
2 The national Ministry of State Organisation intervenes *when the* constitutional *order in* a municipality is *disturbed or threatened and* the affected municipality *cannot protect it itself or with the help of other* municipalities.

---

224 BV Art.50
225 Ministry of State Organisation - 11.5.7 Cultural protection areas for minority protection, Ministry of Free Market Economy - 4 Economic policy, Ministry of Social Market Economy - 4.1 Economic order of the Social Market Economy Ministry of Planned Economy - 4 Social Village Government, Ministry of Barter Economy - 7 Administration of Barter Economy Zones, Ministry of Integration - 6.3 Cultural Protection Area
226 BV Art.52
227 Ministry of State Organisation - 11.2.1 Constitutional Order

3 The foreign ministries shall intervene if the constitutional order in an international ministry is disturbed or threatened and the constitution or laws of a member state are violated.

§132[228] Declaration of general applicability and obligation to participate[229]

1 The nation may *(...)* *declare* national law to be *generally binding or oblige* municipalities to participate *in* inter-municipal treaties in *the following areas of responsibility:*
a. *Execution of sentences and measures;*
b. Degrees in the *school system;*
c. Degrees from colleges*;*
d. *Cultural institutions of supra-regional importance;*
e. *Waste management;*
f. *Wastewater treatment;*
g. Air pollution control;
h. Long-distance traffic;
i. *Cutting-edge medicine and special clinics;*
j. *Institutions for the integration and care of* disabled persons;
k. Basic research and priority research.
2 The same applies to the declaration of general applicability of international law vis-à-vis national and municipal law, provided that the ministries affected are communitarised.
3 *The declaration of general applicability shall take the form of a committee* and subsequent voting.
4 The Ministry of State Organisation shall determine the requirements *for the declaration of general applicability and for the obligation to participate and shall regulate the procedure* in the law.

---

228 BV Art.48a
229 Ministry of State Organisation - 10.1 Subsidiarity principle

§133[230] Precedence and compliance with national law[231]

1 Constitutional law always takes precedence over international, national and municipal law.

2 National law *takes precedence over conflicting* international and municipal *law.*

3 Municipal laws constitute municipal law and may prevail over international or national law.

4 The nation, with the help of national ministers and deputy ministers, *monitors compliance with* national law *by* international ministries or municipalities.

5 The people may allow exceptions by subsidiarity vote.

§134[232] Implementation of the law[233]

1 Municipalities *implement* national or international law in accordance with the constitution *and the law.* Law-making is done by responsible ministers in voting with citizens or councils.

a. Internationally administered ministries implement international law. The deputy ministers in the municipalities put it into practice.

b. Nationally administered ministries implement national law. The deputy ministers in the municipalities put it into practice.

c. Municipally administered ministries implement municipal law. The municipal minister implements the law.

2 The concrete implementation of the law is always done by humans in a place. The place decides which municipality is responsible for implementation.

3 International law replaces national law if the responsible ministry is administered internationally. Municipalities shall only not implement national or international law that conflicts with their municipal laws.

4 National or international ministers and deputy or municipal

---

230 BV Art.49
231 Ministry of State Organisation - 11.2.2 Precedence of law between levels, Ministry of Justice - 4.8 Areas of law
232 BV Art.46
233 Ministry of State Organisation - 11.2.3 Implementation of the law, 11.4.2 International Union, 11.5.2 Municipal level

ministers may agree with each other *that* municipalities *achieve certain objectives in the implementation of* national or international law *and, to this end, carry out programmes which* the ministry concerned finances in whole or in part.

5 The national or international central administration of each ministry leaves *the municipal* ministerial offices as much freedom of design *as possible* so that municipal *specificities are taken into account* and a nationally or internationally comparable similar state service can be provided.

6 The people may, in a subsidiarity vote, order or revoke the authority of the national central administration of a ministry to issue instructions.

Chapter 3: Federal Relations

§135[234] Tasks of the ministries[235]

1 The ministries shall perform *the tasks assigned to* them *by the* Constitution and the population.

2 Ministries can be administered internationally, nationally or municipally. Exceptions are the ministries of security and justice, which cannot be administered municipally.

3 The people decide on the division of responsibilities between the municipality, the nation and the International Union for each ministry in a subsidiarity vote.

§136[236] Relations between nations, nation and municipalities[237]

1 International or national ministers care for heterarchical *relations* between nations or nation and municipalities in their ministry *and* work *with* their deputies in the municipalities.

2 They shall approve *the decrees of the* municipalities *where the implementation of* international or national law so *requires.*

---

234 BV Art.42
235 Ministry of State Organisation - 8.4 Ministries
236 BV Art.186
237 Ministry of State Organisation - 11.2.4 Cooperation of staff between levels in a ministry

3 They may *object to treaties between* municipalities *or* to treaties between municipalities *and foreign countries.*

4 They ensure *compliance with* international or national and municipal law and take *the necessary measures as long as* municipalities do not administer themselves after a subsidiarity vote.

§137 Interaction of national and municipal staff of ministries[238]

1 The level with the largest number of those entitled to vote is above the levels with fewer entitled to vote. Namely, this is the:

a. international level only in the ministry that has been communitarised.

b. national level, if the ministry is not communitarised or municipal self-governing.

c. municipal level, if the ministry's municipal autonomy has been determined in a subsidiarity vote.

2 The way of working is characterised by heterarchy. Superiors are elected by their subordinates. A new election is triggered as soon as more than half of the subordinates demand it. A term-limited rotation principle is also permissible.

3 The highest political level respects organisational autonomy in the areas of accountability of elected politicians within the ministry.

4 The highest political level is not hierarchically above the lower levels, but in a heterarchical alliance. For this purpose, all employees of a ministry jointly draw up a working plan in an alliance, through which all the requirements of the law are fulfilled.

5 Staff at lower levels are allowed to change this working plan if it still meets all the requirements of the law. Different working plans can be used in different municipalities or nations as long as the law requirements are met.

6 All staff members share working strategies for more efficient

---

238 Ministry of State Organisation - 8.4.3.2 Working plan, 11.2.4 Cooperation of staff between levels in a ministry

ways of solving problems in the delivery of state services and thus continuously update the working plan.

7 National or international ministers and their deputies in the municipalities coordinate the process of preparing the working plan and are responsible for its fulfilment in the interest of their constituents.

8 National and international workers work in the ministry's capital city. Municipal workers work in the town halls of the municipalities. Working from home is permissible as long as all necessary services can be provided.

§138[239] Federal relations between several ministries[240]

1 The Ministry of State Organisation provides for the care of relations *between the nation* and municipalities.

2 It ensures the events of several ministries or municipalities and moderates the necessary committees through Federal Moderators.

3 It moderates the negotiation of treaties between municipalities in a committee if the people or affected citizens of a municipality object via the veto quorum.

4 The Ministry of Foreign Affairs assumes these tasks when nation or municipalities cooperate internationally with other nations or municipalities.

§139[241] Treaties between municipalities[242]

1 *The* municipalities may *conclude treaties with each other and establish joint organisations and institutions. They may (...) jointly perform tasks of regional interest* and form alliances.

2 The national or international ministry may participate within the scope of *its responsibilities.*

3 *Treaties between* municipalities shall *not be contrary to the law and interests* of the nation or nations, or to *the rights of*

---

239 BV Art.172
240 Ministry of State Organisation - 11.2 Political levels
241 BV Art.48
242 Ministry of State Organisation - 11.5.6 Cooperation between municipalities

other municipalities. *They shall be* published by the Ministry of Media Affairs.

4 The municipalities *may* establish inter-municipal *bodies by means of an* inter-municipal *treaty*, provided that *the treaty:*
a. has been approved in accordance with the same procedure that applies to legislation;
b. determines the basic content of the provisions.
c. is not contrary to the constitution.
5 The allied municipalities *observe* inter-municipal *law.*
6 Citizens of allied municipalities can use the participation quorum to convene a council of ministers to represent their electoral votes. The council of ministers can be recalled with the same majority.

Chapter 4: Federal Legislation and the Executive

§140 Federal election of persons[243]

1 At the municipal level, either deputy ministers or municipal ministers are:
a. directly elected by citizens of the municipality.
b. elected indirectly by delegated party members or party wing leaders of the municipality if citizens of the municipality have lent out their vote.
c. elected representatively by the party council if at least 90% of the citizens of the municipality have lent out their vote.
2 At the national level, national ministers:
a. directly elected by the people.
b. elected indirectly by delegated party members or party wing leaders when citizens have lent out their vote.
c. elected by the Council of Ministers on a representative basis if a majority of the people vote in favour after a participation quorum and all votes are given to the deputy minister responsible for their municipality.
3 At the international level, international ministers:

---

243 Ministry of State Organisation - 11.3 Responsibilities in federalism, 11.3.1.1 National election of persons, 11.4.2.1 International election of persons, 11.5.3.1 Municipal election of persons

a. directly elected by all affected peoples.

b. elected indirectly by delegated party members or party wing leaders when citizens have lent out their vote.

c. elected by the International Council on a representative basis if a majority of all affected peoples vote in favour after a participation quorum and all votes are given to the ministers responsible for their nation.

4 At all levels, programmes and candidates are formulated by the respective federally responsible committees, parties or councils and put forward for pre-election, selected accordingly and put forward for run-off election.

a. Election programmes are negotiated directly in a Citizens' Committee, People's Committee or Peoples Committee and put to a run-off election.

Candidates are determined directly in a Citizens' Committee, People's Committee or Peoples Committee before the run-off election.

b. Party wings shall draw up their programmes and elect candidates in public meetings. Borrowed votes may only be cast in the pre-election and run-off election ballots, not in the committees.

c. The formulation and combination of election programmes and the selection of candidates is done by the Council of Ministers or the International Council. At the municipal level, the municipal party council can only take on this task if at least 90% of the citizens of the municipality have lent out their vote.

5 All other procedures for the election of persons shall remain the same. More detailed provisions on the election procedure are contained in Articles 59 to 63.

§141 Municipal government[244]

1 Municipal government can arise when one or more municipalities obtain self-government of one or more ministries through a subsidiarity vote.

2 All the procedures referred to in this Article are the same

---

244 Ministry of State Organisation - 8.6.4 Party Council, 11.5.3 Municipal Government

as the centralised procedure in Article 106, except for the
following:
a. Only the people as a whole can give themselves a constitution.
b. If the citizens have chosen the representative form of
government in a vote, the municipal party council publicly
negotiates the wording of the government decision with the
municipal minister on regional state television and takes a
final vote on it.
c. No deputy ministers are elected. Citizens of the municipality
must instead lend out their votes to party members or party
wing leaders of the municipality in order to form a municipal
party council.
3 The ministries of security and justice cannot be governed by
municipalities.

§142[245] Municipal laws[246]

1 Each municipality makes municipal laws for itself in
the ministries that are under its own responsibility after a
subsidiarity vote.
2 Every municipality gives itself a municipal law through a
successful Counter-template.
3 Municipal laws require the consent of the affected population
and must be able to be amended or deleted after a repeal
quorum if requested by a majority *of those entitled to vote.*
4 Municipal laws *require the guarantee* of the nation or nations.
The nation or nations guarantee *them if they do not contradict*
the constitution.

§143 International Government[247]

1 International government can come into being when several
neighbouring countries are in an international union and want
to move from the outer ring to the middle ring. This requires a

---

245 BV Art.51
246 Ministry of State Organisation - 11.5.4 Municipal laws
247 Ministry of State Organisation - 8.6.3 International Council, 11.4
Global policy

subsidiarity vote in which all citizens of those peoples involved are entitled to vote.

2 All the procedures referred to in this Article shall correspond in the same way to the central procedure from Article 106. Exceptions shall apply as follows:

a. Only when all ministries are administered internationally will all peoples give themselves a common constitution and become one people in a new nation.

b. If the citizens have chosen the representative form of government in a vote, the international council shall negotiate publicly on state television of all member states with the international minister the wording of the government decision and take a final vote on it.

c. As long as no international minister has been elected, the elected national ministers of each member state together with their deputies from the municipalities form the international council.

§144 Federal legislation[248]

1 If a ministry is administered municipally, the municipal ministers are responsible in indirect legislation, a citizens' committee in direct legislation and the municipal party council in representative legislation. Representative legislation can only be used in municipal legislation if 90% of the citizens affected have lent out their votes to a party member or party wing. Only then can the municipality's party council have a say and vote on the wording.

2 If a ministry is administered internationally, the international ministers are responsible in indirect legislation, the peoples committee in direct legislation and the international council in representative legislation. All citizens of those nations involved are entitled to vote. If several ministries are involved in an international legislative process that is not administered internationally, laws may only be imported in those countries where at least 75% of the people have given their consent in

---

248 Ministry of State Organisation - 11.3 Responsibilities in federalism, 11.4.2.2 International legislation, 11.5.3.2 Municipal legislation

each case.

3 Committees and voting will be adapted to municipal or international responsibilities so that venues and broadcast areas are easily accessible by affected citizens.

§145 Federal committees[249]

1 Committees are called differently depending on federal responsibility and a smaller or larger group of persons is entitled to vote. Those entitled to vote are
a. in the citizens' committee, all citizens of the municipality.
b. in the People's Committee, all citizens of the country.
c. in the Peoples Committee, all citizens of the member states of the International Union.
2 The election procedure provides for committees to determine the programmes for the pre-election and the candidates for the run-off election. This determines
a. at municipal level, a citizens' committee.
b. at national level, a People's Committee.
c. at international level, a peoples committee.
3 The legislative process provides for committees to turn initiatives from drafts into templates and to negotiate counter-templates. This happens
a. at municipal level in the citizens' committee.
b. at the national level in the People's Committee.
c. at international level in the Peoples Committee.

Title 5: Responsibilities

Chapter 1: Financial regulations

§146[250] Procurement of funds[251]

The state *procures its funds in particular:*
a. by the collection of taxes and fees;

---

249 Ministry of State Organisation - 11.1 Definitions in federalism
250 KV Art.102
251 Ministry of Finance - 8 State revenues

b. from the income of its assets;

c. from profits of the People's Innovation Companies and the ministries.

§147 Profits of the Ministries[252]

1 Ministries may make profits through economic activity. A maximum of 10% profit mark-up may be charged on fees for state services. 50% of the profits are to be transferred to the state budget, 25% as profit sharing for the employees of the ministry and 25% as a share of the profits which remains in the ministry as savings for independent use.

2 ministers distribute the savings from profit shares. The distribution is done publicly on Government Television in the presence of all politicians of a ministry. The politicians can distribute savings:

a. invest in the ministry's infrastructure;

b. use to offset additional costs above the voted level of the past budget vote;

c. continue to save for future projects of the ministry.

3 The savings of the ministries may be paid into the state budget in whole or in part in the course of the budget vote to supplement or replace tax money.

§148[253] Principles of taxation[254]

1 *The design of taxes* is limited to the possibilities of management in the national accounts. Consumption can be regulated through the value added tax. Investment or savings can be regulated via the level of business taxes in the respective economic forms. Other taxes that deviate from this must be voted on by the people.

2 *In the case of* taxes, *the principles of generality, economic* justification, *equality of rights and uniformity of taxation as well*

---

252 Ministry of Finance - 8.4 Profits
253 BV Art.127, KV Art.104
254 Ministry of Finance - 5 Tax policy, 5.2.7 Business taxes in the economic forms, 5.2.7.1 Double taxation, 5.7 Tax auditors of the Company Auditing Agency

*as the principle of taxation according to economic productivity
shall be observed.*
3 A fee for a state service is preferable to a tax wherever possible.
4 The different corporate tax rates in the different economic
forms depend on the extent of state services.
5 *Taxes on* companies shall be set in a way that preserves
*competitiveness and takes into account social benefits and efforts
to ensure full employment.*
6 Domestic *double taxation is prohibited.* The Ministry
of Finance shall take *the necessary measures in voting with*
the responsible Ministries of Labour; Foreign Affairs and
Economy.
7 *Tax evasion and tax fraud shall be effectively punished.* Further
details shall be determined by the Ministry of Justice in voting
with the Ministries of Security, Labour and Finance.

§149[255] Tax harmonisation[256]

1 The Ministry of Finance shall lay down *principles on the
harmonisation of (...) taxes* when switching assets, goods and
services between economic forms.
*2 Harmonisation shall extend to tax liability, the subject matter
and timing of taxes, procedural law and criminal tax law. In
particular, the* type of tax and *the tax rates shall be exempt from
harmonisation.*
3 The Ministry of Finance issues laws against emerging tax
avoidance or tax fraud.

§150 Business taxes[257]

1 The Ministry of Finance collects business taxes in voting
with the ministries of economy.

255 BV Art.129
256 Ministry of Finance - 5.2.7.2 Tax harmonisation
257 Ministry of Finance - 5.2 Business tax, 5.2.7 Business taxes   in
economic forms, 9.5.3.4 Distribution of business taxes, Ministry of
Free Market Economy - 13 Tax policy, Ministry of Social Market
Economy - 10.2 Insolvency insurance, 16 Tax policy, 17.5.7 Downturn
insurance, Ministry of Planned Economy - 6.3.3 Move of entrepreneurs
and companies, 16.1 Business taxes, Ministry of Barter Economy - 15.2

2 A company is any gainful economic activity in which one or more persons are engaged, as well as capital investments in any form.

3 Business taxes increase with the share of state service. They are lowest in the Barter Economy, followed by the Free Market Economy, the Social Market Economy and the Planned Economy.

a. In the Barter Economy, taxes are paid in the form of goods and services managed to sustain the Barter Economy Zones and their natural resources. Existing savings or current income from other economic forms must be deposited with the People's Bank, earn interest there, and each receipt of money is taxed.

b. In the Planned Economy, taxes are paid in the form of labour contributions to basic supply and profit taxes from luxury supply. Existing savings must be invested with the People's Bank and are taxed once when moving in to the Social Village. Current income from other economic forms must be invested with the People's Bank and is taxed annually.

c. In the Social Market Economy, taxes are paid in the form of business taxes on monthly profits and contributions for compulsory insurance. The tax rate includes flat rates for guaranteeing labour protection measures, unemployment insurance, company pension as well as certification of standards for fair trade, ecological production and high quality.

d. In the Free Market Economy, taxes are paid in the form of business taxes on turnover earmarked for the maintenance of ministries and for services provided by the ministries of state organisation, media, family and foreign affairs.

4 The responsible ministries of economy may, in voting with the Ministry of Finance, change tax rates to adjust them to the economic performance of their economic form.

5 All business taxes are settled through a mandatory tax account at People's Bank.

§151[258] Value added tax[259]

1 The Ministry of Finance shall levy a value added tax on supplies of goods *and services (...).*
2 The Ministry of Barter Economy may set a flat rate of working hours for the taxation of value added in the barter economy.[260]
3 The proceeds are saved and are available to the people in the annual budget vote.
4 Adjustments to the VAT rate are voted on by the people in the budget vote by the Ministry of Finance.

§152[261] Tariffs[262]

1 *Legislation on tariffs and other duties on the cross-border movement of goods is the responsibility of* the Ministries of Finance, Labour, Health, Foreign Affairs and Security.
2 Tariffs are levied on all goods and services whose export or import endangers the domestic labour market, environmental or health protection.
3 Tariffs are imposed on all domestic exports or foreign imports that impede the development of the affected industry in a developing country.
4 The amount of the tariffs shall be based on the performance of one of the above tasks.
5 Customs agreements are determined by the Ministry of Foreign Affairs in negotiations with foreign agencies. Any resulting trade agreements and customs regulations shall be submitted to the people for voting.
6 The ministries of economy can levy further tariffs to manage the foreign trade of their economic form.

---

258 BV Art.130
259 Ministry of Finance - 5.1 Value added tax
260 Ministry of Barter Economy - 15.1 Value added taxes
261 BV Art.133
262 Ministry of Finance - 5.3 Tariffs, Ministry of Labour - 10.3.2 Tariffs, Ministry of Health - 4.4.1 Damage limitation, 4.5 Institutes of the Ministry of Health, Ministry of Foreign Affairs - 4.4 Democratic Negotiations, 7.3.13 International Financial Policy, 8.7.1 Import Tariffs, 8.7.2 Export Tariffs, Ministry of Security - 8 Customs

§153[263] Exclusion of double taxation[264]

1 *What* the Ministry of Finance designates *as subject to value added tax* and business tax *or declares to be exempt from tax* shall not be subject to like *taxes.* Tariffs are not managed as taxes.

2 If the responsibilities lie with a municipality, a tax must be collected either at municipal or national level. The affected municipalities regulate their finances in voting with the national Ministry of Finance.

3 If assets, citizens or companies are engaged in different economic forms, the Ministry of Finance, in voting with the Ministry of Labour, shall regulate the transfer between economic forms.[265]

§154 Tax reduction[266]

1 All ministries work entrepreneurially with the people in an economy to generate profits that reduce taxes in return. The Ministry of Finance is responsible for this.

2 All ministries try to price their services with cost-covering fees, which they offer to citizens as individual services or subscriptions. The price surcharge of a maximum of 10% is intended to finance services that cannot be charged as fees without thereby promoting the inheritance of social inequalities. All surpluses of a ministry above 10% must be brought to the next budget vote. In order not to let the profits rise above 10%, the price for the service is to be lowered.

3 The Ministry of Innovation is responsible for the operation of People's Innovation Companies that generate monopoly profits through the exclusive marketing of patent products. People's Innovation Companies whose patents have expired

---

263 BV Art.134
264 Ministry of Finance - 5.2.7.1 Double Taxation, 5.5 Tax Account
265 Ministry of Labour - 10 Freedom of movement between economic forms
266 5.8 Tax reduction, 6 Unconditional Basic Income,- 4.6, Ministry of Social Market Economy -13.4.2 Shares for machinery, 16, Ministry of Planned Economy - 10.7 People's Innovation Companies, 10.9 Research and development, Ministry of Innovation - 10.1 Initiators, 10.4.7 VAT reduction, 10.6 Privatisation,- 4.10.2

are converted into a Social Market Economy joint-stock company. Half of all shares will be distributed to the entire workforce in equal shares. The other half of all shares will be offered for sale to domestic nationals through the People's Bank.

4 The Ministries of Education, Innovation and Planned Economy shall promote inventive activity in their institutions, namely in schools, colleges, research institutes, People's Innovation Companies and Social Villages. Any inventions created within the institutions are protected. There is a legal right to apply for a patent free of charge, but without investigation and examination. All applications are examined to see if a patent could create a successful People's Innovation Company. If this is the case, an offer will be made to the inventors. The offer may include covering the costs of the investigation, legal drafting, examination, worldwide patent application and worldwide marketing, as well as mandatory participation of the inventors in the management of the company or in profits from the product or licence.

5 With the increasing automation of operations, business taxes are increasingly being converted into fees for the operation of machinery to finance an Unconditional Basic Income for all domestic nationals.

§155[267] State expenditure[268]

1 The Ministry of Finance, in voting with all ministries and the taxpayers, *decides on the expenditure of the* state, sets the budget and approves *the state accounts.*

2 It shall, in voting with all ministries, determine an overall financial plan for the distribution of all funds and put it to a vote.

3 It holds the annual budget vote. There, those entitled to vote distribute the saved tax money and other revenues of the ministries for the coming financial year among the ministries.

4 Those entitled to vote can permanently view all cost centres

---

267BV Art. 167

268Ministry of Finance - 9.1.1 Intranet visualisation, 9.2 Cabinet draft budget, 9.5 Budget vote, 11 People's Bank

of the ministries on the intranet. They are able to change the amounts indicated.

5 The Ministry of Finance operates the State Bank, through whose accounts taxpayers must pay their taxes and domestic nationals or companies in the exchange, planned or social market economy can lend out their savings to the state.

6 The Ministry of Finance shall determine further details in the law.

§156[269] Principles for the allocation of tax money[270]

1 The ministries receive their money through the annual budget vote.

2 The community in which the benefit of a state service accrues bears its costs.

3 The community that bears the costs of a state service may determine this service.

4 Basic supply services must be available to all nationals *in a comparable manner.*

5 State tasks must be fulfilled according to need and economically.

§157[271] Budget management[272]

1 The Ministry of Finance shall *keep* the expenditure *and revenues* of all ministries *in balance at* least and at a maximum of 10% profits in the long run.

2 The ministries charge fees for direct services that cover costs and include a maximum of 10% profit. The profits represent equity of the ministries, which may be nationalised by the people through a committee to be used elsewhere by the state.

3 It is inadmissible to finance the state budget through loans. Exceptions must be voted on by the people. Lenders to the state may only be domestic nationals.

---

269 BV Art. 43a

270 Ministry of Finance - 8.7 Principles for the distribution of state revenues, Ministry of State Organisation - 11.4.3 Financing of international ministries

271 BV Art. 126, KV Art.101

272 Ministry of Finance - 7.5 Balancing business cycles, 8.2 fees, 8.4 profits, 8.5 debts, 9 state expenditure, 9.7 Audit Court

4 The *financial budget shall be managed economically, sparingly and in accordance with the economic cycle and the originator.*
5 The Ministry of Finance shall undertake comprehensive financial planning *and shall, as far as possible, coordinate it with the financial planning* of the ministries.
6 *Before taking on a new task, it must be explained how it can be financed.*
7 *All tasks shall be reviewed* in the course of the annual budget vote for their necessity *and appropriateness as well as for their financial impact and their sustainability.*
8 The budget for the coming year is saved in the current year. If higher costs are incurred than voted, the missing amount is taken from the savings for the coming financial year. Ministers who incur costs in excess of the agreed level must spend the ministry's assets on them or be liable for them, or a supplementary budget is passed in a committee.

§158[273] Ministry finances[274]

1 Ministers annually develop a financial *plan* for the coming year for their ministry, draft *the budget*, prepare the national *accounts* and submit the financial plan to the people for an annual budget vote.
2 They shall ensure proper *financial management* in their ministry.
3 The ministries of finance and labour monitor proper budget management and inform the population of their results and publish the data.

§159 Budget vote[275]

1 The Ministry of Finance holds an annual budget vote in which citizens can vote on the distribution of state revenues to ministries.

---

273 BV Art.183
274 Ministry of Finance - 5.7 Company Auditing Agency tax auditors, 9.1 Financial plans of the ministries, 9.7 Audit Court, Ministry of Labour - 20.7.1.2 Tax audit in ministries, 20.7.3.1 State audit
275 Ministry of Finance - 9.5 Budget vote

2 The uses of state revenues for the current fiscal year are proposed in the annual budget vote by the ministries and citizens and voted on for the coming fiscal year.

3 The state budget is saved over one year and spent in the following year. The cut-off date is after the budget vote.

4 In the course of a budget vote, the people have the right to use any assets of their state in accordance with the will of the people.

5 The Ministry of Finance shall regulate the details in the law on budget votes.

§160[276] Financial Supervisory Authority[277]

1 The Financial Supervisory Authority of the state must be ensured *by independent control bodies.* These are the citizens through the intranet and the budget votes, the monitoring team of Surveillance Television and the Company Auditing Agency as well as the Audit Court. Further control bodies can be appointed at the request of 10% of the citizens entitled to vote.

2 The Ministry of Finance shall *regulate the Financial Supervisory Authority of the organisations and persons receiving state services.*

3 Every expenditure requires a legal basis, *a binding* cost estimate, as well as a spending decision by the responsible ministry before it can be approved by the people in the budget vote.

4 The Ministry of Labour supervises the finance economy. It issues basic laws that apply to financial enterprises of all economic forms. These are namely banks, stock exchanges and insurance companies. The laws and their regular review are intended to ensure that the finance economy does not run counter to the common good.

---

276 KV Art.105, 106

277 Ministry of Finance - 9.7 Audit Court, Ministry of Labour - 18.3 Financial Supervisory Authority, 20.7.1.2 Tax audit in ministries, Ministry of Digital Affairs - 15.2 Tax game, Ministry of Media - 12 Surveillance Television

§161[278] Financial and burden equalisation[279]

1 The Ministry of Finance shall issue *regulations on appropriate financial and burden sharing between the* nation *and municipalities*, between municipalities and *between economic forms*.

2 The financial equalisation scheme shall in particular:

a. reduce the differences in financial productivity between municipalities and *economic forms;*

b. ensure minimal financial resources to municipalities and *economic forms;*

c. offset excessive financial burdens on municipalities and *economic forms due to their geographical (...) or socio-demographic conditions;*

d. promote (...) cooperation between municipalities and burden-sharing *economic forms;*

e. maintain the tax competitiveness of the Free Market Economy *in international relations.*

3 The funds for resource equalisation are provided by the resource-rich municipalities and economic forms to the national Ministry of Finance.

4 The ministries of labour and media monitor indigence for financial and burden sharing. The Ministry of Labour uses the expertise of the Company Auditing Agency. The Ministry of Media Affairs uses the monitoring team of Surveillance Television for this purpose. The ministries, in voting with the people, develop measures to make financial and burden sharing superfluous in the medium term. If this has not happened after 20 years, the administrative sovereignty of the affected municipality or economic form can be withdrawn and exercised within the framework of popular empowerment.

5 The Ministry of State Organisation shall determine the details of popular empowerment in a law.

---

278 BV Art. 135

279 Ministry of Finance - 7 Budget consolidation, Ministry of Labour - 20.7.1.2 Tax auditing in ministries, 9.6 Revitalisation and decommissioning of economic systems, 9.7 Balancing between economic forms, Ministry of State Organisation - 12.3 Popular empowerment, Ministry of Media - 12 Surveillance Television

Chapter 2: Foreign countries

§162[280] Foreign affairs[281]

1 Foreign affairs are the responsibility of the Ministry of Foreign Affairs.
2 The Ministry of Foreign Affairs *is committed to unification* with neighbouring countries where the standard of living is the same and where both peoples agree to unification.
3 It advocates the conclusion of treaties between domestic and foreign ministries to be submitted to the voting of the two peoples. Citizens of all participating states are to be involved in the negotiation process in the same way as domestic citizens.
4 It safeguards the welfare of municipalities with Barter Economy, Planned Economy and Social Market Economy from lawless international competition by strictly shifting such business to the Free Market Economy.
5 It contributes to the development of neighbouring states and continents with weaker development through development aid. Development aid is limited to infrastructure and education. The Ministry of Foreign Affairs determines the provisions for further aid in the law.
6 It is responsible for assessing the safety of countries of origin from which asylum applicants come, the asylum application procedure and the deportation procedure. In doing so, it *takes account of the* municipalities *and protects their interests.*

§163[282] Relations with foreign countries[283]

1 The minister of the Ministry of Foreign Affairs shall be responsible for foreign affairs while respecting *the rights of participation of the* other ministries, of his or her own people

---

280 BV Art. 54
281 Ministry of Foreign Affairs - 4 Foreign Affairs, 4.7.3.6 Deportations, 5.4 Free Trade Agreements, 5.8.2 Three Rings of Integration, 7.3.11 International Economic Policy, 8.4 Operation Sites, 9 Asylum Application Procedures
282 BV Art.184
283 Ministry of Foreign Affairs - 4 Foreign Affairs, 4.1 International Treaties, 5 Communitarisation, 5.8 International Union

and, where appropriate, of the foreign peoples.

2 He or she shall sign *the* international treaties *and ratify them in voting with* the people. *He or* she shall *submit them to* the responsible ministries *for approval* and to the people for a vote.

3 If the protection of the country's interests so requires, the Minister for Foreign Affairs may issue regulations. *Regulations shall be limited in time* until they are approved by responsible ministers or the people.

4 Treaties between states or states and foreign companies must be filmed and broadcast and then put to a vote of the domestic people. The foreigner people can also be called upon to vote by domestic law. If the treaty is to be concluded, more than 65% of those entitled to vote must be in favour. Details of the procedure are set out by the Ministry of Foreign Affairs in the law.

5 If an International Union enters into force with one or more other neighbouring states, the International Union shall assume moderation between the involved ministries of the member states. Details of the procedure shall be determined by the Ministry of Foreign Affairs in the law.

§164[284] Participation of citizens in foreign policy decisions[285]

1 Citizens participate in *the preparation of foreign policy decisions.*

2 The Ministry of Media Affairs shall *inform* citizens in a *timely and comprehensive manner and seek their opinions.*

3 The opinions of citizens are of *particular importance if they are affected in their* personal or professional interests. *In these cases,* as many of the citizens affected as possible participate *in international negotiations* through a committee.

4 A veto quorum can be used to obtain direct democratic participation in the negotiations by citizens.

284BV Art. 55
285Ministry of Foreign Affairs - 4.4 Democratic Negotiations

§165[286] Relations of municipalities with foreign countries[287]

1 The municipalities may *conclude treaties with foreign countries in their areas of accountability.*
2 These treaties shall not be contrary to the law and interests of the nation *and the rights of other* municipalities. *The* municipalities *shall inform* the people with the help of the Ministry of Media Affairs *before concluding the treaties.* Citizens have the opportunity to see the progress of the contract negotiations at any time. A veto quorum allows for direct democratic participation in the negotiations by citizens.
3 Municipalities *can deal directly with subordinate foreign authorities*, but must always publish their activities for citizens as video and text on the intranet.

§166[288] Relations with foreign countries and treaties under international law[289]

1 The Ministry of Foreign Affairs, in voting with the people and affected ministries, shall *be involved in the formulation of foreign policy and shall* ensure *the care of relations with foreigners.*
2 It approves treaties under international law, with the exception of treaties *for the conclusion of which deputy* foreign ministers of the municipalities are responsible under the law *or an international treaty.*
3 The Ministry of Foreign Affairs tries to conclude as many peace treaties as possible with other countries.

§167[290] Implementation of international law treaties[291]

1 Treaties under international law shall be subject to *mandatory* referendums.

---

286 BV Art. 56
287 Ministry of Foreign Affairs - 4.4 Democratic Negotiations
288 BV Art.166
289 Ministry of Foreign Affairs - 4 Foreign Affairs, 5.3 Peace Treaties, 7.2 International Law
290 BV Art. 141a
291 Ministry of Foreign Affairs - 7.2 International law, Ministry of State

2 Treaties under international law are subject to a repeal quorum.

3 If an international law treaty is not in conformity with the constitution, a constitutional committee shall put *the constitutional amendments serving the implementation of the treaty* to a vote of the people.

4 If an international law treaty is not in accordance with the law, a committee shall put *the amendments to the law that serve the implementation of the treaty* to a vote of the people.

§168[292] World peace[293]

1 The peoples should be allowed to discuss conflicts with each other and, if necessary, to demarcate themselves in cultural protection areas in order to avoid war.

2 The Ministry of Foreign Affairs shall work for unification with states that grant their citizens the rights of this Constitution, are contiguous to the borders of the country with this Constitution and offer the same standard of living.

3 The Ministry of Foreign Affairs is committed to the unification of states that grant their citizens direct democratic constitutional law and are located on foreign continents or in distant cultural areas.

4 The Ministry of Foreign Affairs aims at the united states of the continent in the short term, the unification of states on the continents in the medium term and the unification of all united states of the continents into the united states of the world in the long term.

5 The Ministry of Foreign Affairs loses its basis for existence on the day on which the united states of the world are proclaimed. Only the discovery of extraterrestrial intelligent life forms then provides a basis for the existence of a Ministry of Foreign Affairs again.

6 The constitution of the united states of the world must

Organisation - 9.6.2.3 Mandatory committees, 9.7.4 Mandatory voting

292 BV Art. 173

293 Ministry of Foreign Affairs - 5 Communitarisation, 5.3 Peace Treaties, 6.5 United states of the continent, 7.2.8 International Disputes, 7.4 United States of the Continents, 7.5.2 Long-term Perspective, 10 End of the Ministry of Foreign Affairs

enshrine dynamic democracy, a ban on war among humans and a ban on killing humans. Suicide remains permissible.

7 The Ministry of Foreign Affairs undertakes peaceful measures to safeguard the country's *external security, independence, neutrality*, conclusion of peace treaties and international or supranational networking.

Chapter 3: Security, national defence, civil defence

§169[294] Security[295]

1 The Minister of Security shall take measures to safeguard the *internal and external security, independence and* military *neutrality* of the country.

2 The Ministry of Security shall, *within* its responsibilities, ensure the *security of the country and the protection of the population.*

3 It coordinates its *efforts in the area of internal security* with all municipalities.

4 It also coordinates its law enforcement efforts with foreign police services.

5 It shall maintain the armed security agencies, namely the army, Customs, police and People's Protection Service, as well as the unarmed security agencies, namely the fire brigade, rescue service and Technical Relief Agency.

6 It brings offenders to the responsible courts through its agencies, working with the Public Prosecutor's Office of the Ministry of Justice.

7 It coordinates its efforts in the field of external security with all nations involved in the Continental Defence Army or in defence installations against celestial bodies in Earth orbit.

---

294 BV Art. 173, 57
295 Ministry of Security - 3 Tasks of the Ministry of Security, 4.6 Security Directory, 5 Prevention of danger, 7 Police, 7.3 Digital police files, 7.4 Investigation Directory, 9 Military

§170 Moral courage[296]

1 Inland, all persons have the right to inform other persons of violations of the law or constitutional articles. If there is a risk of absconding, provisional arrest is permissible. The Ministry of Security regulates the details of provisional arrest in the law.
2 Inland, all persons are obliged to provide first aid to humans. Anyone who threatens to put themselves in danger must immediately notify the security agencies.

§171[297] Civil defence[298]

1 Legislation on civil protection for the prevention of danger to *persons and property (...) is the responsibility of the Ministry of Security.*
2 It shall issue *regulations on the deployment of civil defence in the event of disasters and emergencies.* It shall operate the civil defence bodies, namely the fire brigade, rescue services and Technical Relief Agency, with honorary volunteers or salaried employees.
3 It shall issue *regulations on the appropriate compensation for loss of earnings* for volunteers.
4 Persons performing protective service who suffer damage to their *health or lose their lives are entitled to appropriate assistance* from the Ministry of Security *for themselves or their dependants.*

§172[299] Internal and external security in a state of emergency[300]

1 A state of emergency is declared when citizens or state employees have to act in self-defence in order to avert a state-threatening situation caused by humans. The state of

296 Ministry of Security - 4.1 Security forces, 4.9 Demonstrations, 5.2 Rescue service, 5.3 Fire brigade, 5.4 Technical Relief Agency, 5.6 Emergency number 110, 6.4 Patrol service for the police including social services
297 BV Art. 61
298 Ministry of Security - 5 Prevention of danger, 5.2 Rescue service, 5.3 Fire service, 5.4 Technical Relief Agency
299 KV Art. 91
300 Ministry of Security - 4.10 state of emergency, 5.7.3 emergency plan,

emergency serves to avert *serious disturbances of public order* or internal or external *security that have occurred or are imminent.*

2 Depending on the event, different ministries are responsible for regularisation and implementation of the measures to be taken with the citizens in the state of emergency.

a. In the event of war, the Ministry of Security is responsible for waging war and the Ministry of Foreign Affairs conducts negotiations to end the war. The people retain supreme command over the military and the negotiations. It decides at any time whether to continue or end the war by a quorum. The population is to be armed in the event of war.

b. In the event of civil war, the Ministry of Security is responsible for separating, disarming, arresting and reconciling the parties to the civil war.

c. In the event of a revolt, the Ministry of Security is responsible for stopping rioting and terrorism. The Ministry of State Organisation is responsible for putting government decisions up for discussion and determining minority and majority ratios and finding solutions to end the revolt.

d. In the event of a coup, the Ministry of State Organisation is responsible for organising governance at national or municipal level in order to deprive the insurgents of power over jurisdictions they are trying to seize. The Ministry of Security shall ensure the capture of areas occupied by insurgents, their disarmament and arrest.

e. In the event of a coup d'état, mayors are responsible for organising governance at municipal level in order to deprive the insurgents of power over responsibilities. The population is to be armed. They form vigilantes to defend and control the territory of the municipality. Municipality vigilantes join together to form armed combat units to fight insurgents.

3 The Ministry of Security is entitled to deploy military troops domestically in cases a. to d. to deploy military troops inland. In case e. this responsibility lies in municipal self-administration. The mayors shall work with the citizens in accordance with established procedures. The procedures to be followed are

---

7.10 riot, 7.12 city raid, 9 military, 9.4 soldiers, 9.4.1 basic training, 9.5 warfare, 9.5.2 coup, 9.5.3 defensive war, Ministry of State Organisation - 12.7 state of emergency, 12.7.7 coup d'état

determined by the Ministry of State Organisation in the law.
4 If the deployment of the military at home or abroad is expected to last longer than 2 weeks, a committee must be convened immediately. In the event of war, a voting on continuation or surrender must take place at least every 3 months.

§173[301] Army[302]

1 The state shall maintain an *army. This is organised according to the militia principle* and is only deployed in the event of national defence. Soldiers have regular jobs and attend regular military training. For this time they receive military pay.

2 The armed forces serve to prevent war and contribute to maintaining border security. Foreign missions are prohibited. *It defends the country and its population. It supports the civil authorities in warding off serious threats to internal security and in dealing with other extraordinary situations.* The Ministry of Security may provide for *other tasks in the law.*

3 The Ministry of Security seeks peace treaties and treaties on joint armies with neighbouring and allied states in order to be able to jointly defend the external borders.

4 The use of *the army is a matter for* the nation. Within 2 weeks of the start of a war, the people must vote on whether to continue the war. As long as the war is going on, veto quorums can be triggered at any time, in which the people negotiate tactics with the Ministry of Security. The people can surrender at any time to end a war.

5 The Ministry of Security *orders* military service *and provides the army or parts thereof for this purpose.*

---

301 BV Art. 58, 173
302 Ministry of Security - 3 Tasks of the Ministry of Security, 7.10 Rioting, 7.12 City raids, 8.2 Border protection 9 Military, 9.3.1 Continental Defence Army, 9.4.1 Basic training, 9.5 Warfare

§174[303] Military and People's Service[304]

1 Every domestic citizen *is obliged to perform military service.* Those who do not wish to perform service with weapons are trained for military duties without weapons.

2 Military service consists of three months of basic military training for national defence.

3 The People's Service consists of nine months' work in a maximum of three different state work areas. The ministries advertise suitable positions.

4 The Ministry of Security shall issue *regulations on reasonable compensation for loss of earnings.*

5 Persons performing military or People's Service who suffer damage to their *health or lose their lives are entitled to appropriate assistance* from the Ministry of Security *for themselves or their dependants.*

§175[305] Organisation, training and equipment of the armed forces[306]

1 Military legislation as well as the organisation, training and equipment of the armed forces are the responsibility of the Ministry of Security.

2 The Ministry of Security may station *military institutions* in any necessary municipality for adequate *compensation.*

3 The Ministry of Security can share the organisation, training and equipment of the army with allied neighbouring states. For this to happen, a majority of all affected peoples must vote in favour.

4 The Ministry of Security, together with as many states on Earth as possible, shall establish an effective geostationary defence mechanism in Earth orbit against celestial bodies.

---

303 BV Art. 59
304 Ministry of Security - 9.4 Soldiers, 9.4.1 Basic Education, Ministry of Education - 10 People's Service
305 BV Art. 60
306 Ministry of Security - 9.3.1 Continental Defence Army, 9.4.2 Weapon Systems

Chapter 4: Education, research and culture

§176[307] **Education space**[308]

1 The Ministry of Education ensures *high quality and permeability of the education area within the scope of* its responsibilities. To this end, it coordinates teaching content with the ministries of labour and innovation.

2 All educational institutions shall *coordinate their efforts and ensure their cooperation through joint bodies and other arrangements.*

3 *In fulfilling their tasks, they shall work to ensure that general education and vocational education and training pathways receive equal recognition.*

4 In the education area, all qualifications are completed according to a national standard and with uniform final examinations.

5 The educational institutions shall promote *the harmonious development of physical, mental,* creative, innovative, *emotional and social abilities, as well as a sense of responsibility towards humans* and the *environment.*

§177[309] **School system**[310]

1 *The Ministry of Education* is responsible for the school system. It runs state nursery schools, schools and colleges and ensures that *all* citizens receive *adequate* education.

2 It ensures democratic participation of all teachers and learners in the state educational institutions. It respects the self-determination of the learners with regard to the method, the course association and the timetable. It prepares curricula

307 BV Art. 61a, KV Art.42
308 Ministry of Education - 4.2 Central education system, 4.5 Education Authority, 4.6 Examinations Office, 4.8 Recognition of qualifications, 4.8.1 Domestic recognition, 5 Educational institutions, 5.2 Harmonisation, 8.6.1 Transfer, 9.19 Final examinations, 11.6.8 Higher education qualifications
309 BV Art. 62, KV Art.43
310 Ministry of Education - 4.4.2 Curriculum development, 4.8.1 Domestic citizens' recognition, 5 Educational institutions, 5.2 Harmonisation, 5.3 School law, 5.4 Compulsory education, 5.10 Rights for learners, 6 Special school,

in cooperation with teachers, learners, companies and the ministries of labour, economy and innovation.

3 It shall _supervise public schools and private instruction._

4 Final examinations are issued for all educational institutions by the central office of the Ministry of Education.

5 _At_ state _schools_ and colleges, education _is free of charge_, Tax-funded and _denominationally and politically neutral._

6 The Social Villages shall provide adequate special schooling for _all disabled children and youths up to the_ age _of 20 at the latest._

7 If _no harmonisation of the school system in the area of school entry age and compulsory schooling, the duration and objectives of the educational levels and their transitions as well as the recognition of qualifications is achieved through coordination,_ the national central office of the Ministry of Education shall issue _the necessary regulations._

8 Education is compulsory from the age of six to eighteen.

§178[311] Training contributions[312]

1 Privately operated educational institutions of the free and social market economy may _establish educational contributions._

2 The Ministry of Education does not levy education contributions, but is Tax-funded. In the annual budget vote, the people can determine the amount of tax money. This does not apply to vocational education and training for companies in the Free Market Economy, which is Fee-funded.

3 Education is allowed to generate returns through entrepreneurial co-production as a practical exercise in the classroom.

4 Foreigners must pay education contributions. The amount is determined democratically by each educational institution. At least cost coverage must be ensured. Tuition is only granted to foreigners if there is no waiting list for nationals in this class.

---

311 BV Art.66

312 Ministry of Education - 4.3 Financing, Ministry of Free Market Economy - 14.2.5 Ministry of Education, Ministry of Social Market Economy - 11.2.2 Private educational institutions

§179[313] Promotion of children and youths[314]

1 The Ministry of Education shall take into account *the special support and protection needs of children and youths in the fulfilment of* its tasks.
2 The Ministry of Family Affairs describes the best interests of the child in the law. It maintains the Youth Welfare Office to promote and monitor implementation.
3 The Ministry of Family Affairs, through the Youth Welfare Office, supports parents in the parenting and training of children through a parenting licence, offers of training and advice.
4 It may *support out-of-school work with* parents, *children and youths in addition to* the *measures* of the Ministry of Education, if professionals advise it, the minor requests it, at least one parent wishes it or courts order it.

§180[315] Schools and colleges[316]

1 The Ministry of Education shall operate *the state* schools and *colleges* democratically with equal participation of teachers and learners. It *may establish, take over or operate other* schools, *colleges*, institutes *and other institutions of higher education.*
2 The ministries of education, innovation and labour shall jointly *coordinate and ensure quality assurance in the domestic* school system. In *doing so, they shall take into account the* democratic *autonomy of* teachers and learners *and ensure equal treatment of institutions with the same tasks.*
3 *If* the Ministries of Education, Innovation and Labour

---

313 BV Art.67
314 Ministry of Education - 5.5 Children and Youths, Ministry of Family Affairs - 7.6 Youth Welfare Office, 7.6.2 Behaviour in the event of risk to children's well-being, 7.7.1 Parenting licence, 8.1 Children's rights, Ministry of Justice - 8.4.3 Criminal responsibility.
315 BV Art. 63a, KV Art.44
316 Ministry of Social Market Economy - 17.3 Educational institutions and companies, 17.3.6 Research assignments, Ministry of Planned Economy - 18.2 Education policy, 18.2.7 External in-service training, Ministry of Education - 4.7 Institute of Education, 4.8 Recognition of degrees, 4.9.2 Cooperation between educational institutions and companies, 5 Educational institutions, 5.10 Rights for learners, 11 College, Ministry of Labour - 11.2.1 Necessary educational content, Ministry of Innovation - 6 Innovation through Education

do not achieve *the common objectives through coordination,* the national Ministry of Education shall issue *regulations, on* school-leaving qualifications, *on learning* levels *and their transitions, on continuing education and on the recognition of educational institutions and qualifications.*

4 The Ministry of Education may tie support for the colleges *to uniform funding principles and make it dependent on the division of tasks between the colleges in particularly cost-intensive areas.*

5 Schools and colleges *<u>fulfil their tasks in the service of the general public.</u>*

6 *<u>They promote scientific knowledge through teaching and research and provide services to companies in</u>* the Planned Economy and Social Market Economy.

7 The ministries of Education, Innovation, Planned Economy and Social Market Economy determine further details in the law.

§181[317] Vocational training[318]

1 The Ministry of Education shall issue *regulations on vocational education and training.*

2 It *promotes a broad and permeable range of VET programmes.*

3 It regularly exchanges information on the needs of all companies of all economic forms and integrates them into teaching. To this end, the Ministry of Education cooperates with the Ministries of Labour, Economy and Innovation.

---

317 BV Art. 63

318 Ministry of Free Market Economy - 6.2 Business cooperation, Ministry of Social Market Economy - 17.3.3 Work assignments, Ministry of Planned Economy - 18.2 Education policy, Ministry of Barter Economy - 16.4 Education, Ministry of Education - 4.4.2 Curriculum development, 4.9 Education through work, 11.3 Vocational training college, Ministry of Labour - 11.2 Vocational training, Ministry of Innovation - 6.2 Business cooperation

§182[319] Continuing education[320]

1 The Ministry of Education, in voting with the Ministries of Media, Digital, Innovation, Labour and Economic Affairs, shall *establish principles on continuing education.*
2 It promotes continuing *education* by offering all state teaching content and educational qualifications as distance learning at all times. To this end, the Ministry of Education cooperates with the Ministries of Media and Digital Affairs.
3 The Ministry of Education *specifies the areas of* education and the graduation criteria in the law.

§183[321] Research and innovation[322]

1 The ministries of education, labour and innovation promote *scientific research and innovation.*
2 In *particular,* they may *make funding conditional on quality assurance and coordination being ensured* and on People's Innovation Companies being established and generating profits.
3 They may establish, *take over or operate research facilities*, namely institutes, schools and colleges. The research facilities

---

319 BV Art. 64a
320 Ministry of Free Market Economy - 14.2.5.2 Vocational training, Ministry of Social Market Economy - 17.3.2 Further education, Ministry of Planned Economy - 18.2.1 Education and further education as basic supply work , Ministry of Barter Economy - 16.4 Education, Ministry of Education - 12 Free Education, 12. 4 Digitalised Education, 12.7 Knowledge VZ, Ministry of Labour - 12.2.2 Further Education, Ministry of Innovation - 6.4 Invention Studies, 6.5 Mobile Innovation Labs, Ministry of Media Affairs - 13 Educational Television (BF), Ministry of Digital Affairs - 10.2.1 Knowledge.vz, 13.6.9 Extensions, 15.8 Learning Game
321 BV Art. 64
322 Ministry of Education - 4.7 Institute of Education, 4.10.2 Inventive activity, 4.10.3 Innovative activity in alliance, 9.15.2.8 Physics, 11.7.2 State research institutes, 11.7.4 Research projects with companies, Ministry of Labour - 20.7.5 Innovation auditor, 20.7.5.4.1 Approval of money from the Innovation Fund, Ministry of Innovation - 5 Research and development, 5. 3.1 Research Cost Fund, 5.4 State Research Projects, 5.4.7 Basic Research, 6 Innovation through Education, 6.4 Invention Studies, 6.5 Mobile Innovation Labs, 7.1 Institute of Technology, 9 Innovation Promotion, 9.11.1.1 Innovation Fund, 10.1 Initiators, 10.4.3 Maximising Profits

can be used to work in alliance in order to develop an area of innovation more quickly.

4 They can enter into co-production with domestic citizens. This includes the production of goods parts in class and the education of industrial communities for smooth supply to People's Innovation Companies.

5 They support inventive citizens by simply granting industrial property rights and operating a fund to promote market access. The fund is open to all domestic inventors who undertake to pay 5% of their annual profits into the fund from which they initially drew their start-up capital in the event of profitable marketing from the fifth year onwards.

6 Educational institutions and research institutes participate in basic research.

7 The Ministry of Innovation sets national research tasks for the population. These tasks consist of technical challenges faced by many companies in the domestic economy.

8 All companies can tender for research tasks and pay money into the Research Cost Fund. This fund pools the research expenditures of many companies and is used to pay researchers to complete research tasks.

9 All domestic nationals should have the opportunity to use the state of the art. To this end, the Ministry of Innovation operates mobile laboratories with up-to-date equipment for the production of innovative goods, services or the implementation of research projects.

10 The Ministry of Innovation shall lay down in the law more detailed provisions on the promotion of innovation through the funds for market access promotion and research tasks.

§184[323] Promotion of music, sport, film, culture and art[324]

1 The ministries of family, media and education *promote* music and dance among the population and *the musical education (...) of children, youths* and the gifted.

323 BV Art.67a, 68, 69, 71
324 Ministry of Education - 8.7.4.7 Arts, 8.7.4.8 Sports, 8.7.4.9 Music, 8.8.3.1.1 Project example: producing film, 9.15.2.3 Sports, 9.15.2.5 Music, 9.15.2.18 Arts, 11.5 College and Educational Television, Ministry of Family Affairs - 9 Leisure, 9.2 Music, 9.3 Sports

2 The ministries of family, health and education shall promote *sport, especially training* and exercise. The Ministry of Education may issue *regulations on youth sports and declare physical education in schools to be* compulsory. The municipalities shall create opportunities for sport and recreation in public spaces.[325]

3 The ministries of media and education promote the training and practice of domestic *film production and film culture.* They ensure that citizens know how content is filmed and facilitate co-productions with state television. The state media ensure transparency in state decisions, information about state projects, opportunities for citizens to participate, and diversity *and quality of film offerings.*[326]

4 The ministries of family and integration are responsible *for the area of culture.* They determine together with the people which goods and activities belong to the general cultural property and which subcultures can or should be practised in cultural protection areas. They can run and promote cultural events. They promote the integration of foreign immigrants and immigrants in the sense of integration or assimilation and in doing so pay attention to the interests of the respective municipality.[327]

5 The ministries of education and family shall promote the training and practice of the *arts* and artistic craftspersons.

§185[328] Languages[329]

1 The official language shall be the national language.

2 The respective municipalities may each additionally designate a further official language of their own which shall apply in their territory.

3 In the event of unification with other states, the previous

---

325 Ministry of Health - 6.2 Exercise
326 Ministry of Media - 11 Nationwide Citizen Television, 14 Youth Television
327 Ministry of Integration - 6 Integration, 7.7 Integration measures
328 BV Art.70
329 Ministry of Foreign Affairs - 6.5.2 Cultural Integration, 7.3.4.4 World Language, Ministry of Integration - 6.1 Official Languages, 7.7.1 Language Teaching, Ministry of State Organisation - 4.1.4 National Language

national language shall be the official language inland until 95% of the citizens have mastered the new language. Time limits are only permissible over generations. In the case of a new union of states, a new language should be developed that has similarities with as many languages from the union of states as possible.

4 Translators shall be paid by the person who does not speak the official language.

§186 Peaceful separation[330]

1 Those who stand out among their fellow citizens should be able to cluster with other fellow citizens who stand out in the same or similar ways.

2 The Ministries of Economy, Integration and Infrastructure shall create economic, cultural, legal and local conditions for demarcation.

3 Niches are to be created for each opposition or subculture in which they may carry out their way of life as they wish, as long as all those affected declare their consent by democratic voting. Damage to third parties or the environment as well as violation of the constitution is inadmissible.

§187[331] Separation of church and state[332]

1 The Ministry of Integration is responsible for the regularisation of the relationship *between church and state.*

2 Within the scope of its responsibility, it may take measures *to preserve public peace between the members of the various religious communities.*

3 The roles of state and church are separated. Laicism prevails.

---

330 Ministry of Free Market Economy - 5 Switching between economic forms, Ministry of Social Market Economy - 6.3 Business philosophy, Ministry of Planned Economy - 6.1 Entrance into Planned Economy, 12.3.2 Orientation, Ministry of Barter Economy - 6.1 Area, Ministry of Integration - 6.3 Cultural protection area, Ministry of Infrastructure - 5.4 Building permits.
331 BV Art. 72
332 Ministry of Integration - 6.4 Religious Communities, 6.5.1 Secularism, 6.5.2 Constitutional Fidelity

4 The municipal and national populations may impose rules of conduct on religious communities that preserve public peace.

§188[333] Statistics[334]

1 The ministries shall collect *the necessary statistical data on the state and development of the population, economy, society, education, research, space and environment inland* and administer the data through the Ministry of Digital Affairs.

2 The Ministry of Digital Affairs may issue *regulations on the harmonisation and maintenance of official registers in order to minimise the collection burden.*

3 The Ministry of Education collects surveys on learning success in class.[335]

4 The Ministry of Labour collects economic indicators and employee satisfaction data through the Company Auditing Agency.[336]

5 The Ministry of Integration collects data on the number of foreigners and supraregional moves inland.[337]

6 The Ministry of Family Affairs collects data on the birth rate, death rate and suicide rate.[338]

7 The Ministry of Innovation collects data on the newly filed industrial property rights and inventions of citizens.[339]

8 Each ministry must have at least one intranet site. In addition, ministries can provide citizens with information on work and data management via a directory. They also give citizens the opportunity to view and add to their data via profiles in all directories and to limit the visibility for non-state users.

9 Each ministry may arrange for further data collection in the law.

---

333 BV Art. 65
334 Ministry of Digital Affairs - 6 Statistical Office, 12 Directories
335 Ministry of Education - 4.7.4 Learner Survey, 5.9 Education Directory
336 Ministry of Labour - 20.8 Audit
337 Ministry of Integration - 5 Integration Agency, 7.4 Quota of foreigners
338 Ministry of Family Affairs - 6 Registry Office
339 Ministry of Innovation - 7.3 Patent Office

Chapter 5: Environment and spatial planning

§189[340] Sustainability[341]

1 All citizens and ministries strive for *a sustainable relationship between nature and its capacity for renewal on the one hand, and its use by humans on the other.*
2 All ministries ensure through appropriate laws that future generations can maintain the same standard of living.
3 The Ministry of Health shall supervise compliance with sustainable environmental protection to preserve the health of humans and nature. Hazards are researched by the ministry and made harmless through regulations in the law. All other ministries are obliged to cooperate.

§190[342] Environmental protection[343]

1 The natural environment shall be preserved healthy for present and future generations. It shall be burdened only regeneratively *by state and private activities.*
2 The natural foundations of life may only be burdened to the *extent that their ability to be renewed and their availability continue to be guaranteed.*
3 The Ministry of Health shall issue *regulations* in the law *on the protection of humans and their natural environment from harmful or nuisance effects.*
4 It shall *ensure that such impacts are avoided. The costs of*

---

340 BV Art. 73
341 Ministry of Health - 6.5.1 Sustainability, 6.7.2.1 Circular economy
342 KV Art.31, 36, BV Art.74, KV Art.32
343 Ministry of Health - 4.4.1 Damage limitation, 6.5.2 Nature reserves, 6.6 Environmental protection, 6.7.2.1 Circular economy, Ministry of Infrastructure - 4.1 Homeland protection, 4.2 Environmental protection, 4.9.2 Waste disposal, Ministry of Innovation - 5.4.1 Provision for the future, 9.10.3 Environmental innovations, Ministry of Labour - 14.3 Environmental protection, 14.4 Circular economy, 20.7.2.2 Environmental protection audit, Ministry of Free Market Economy - 6.2 Duties for companies, Ministry of Social Market Economy - 6.7 Environmental protection, Ministry of Planned Economy - 7.2 Occupational health and safety of all work areas, 10.5.7.3 Upgrading company, Ministry of Barter Economy - 9.4 Environmental compatibility

prevention and elimination shall be borne by the originators. It shall *also ensure protection against possible hazards of genetic engineering processes or products.*

5 The Ministry of Infrastructure works to reduce *water pollution and ensures that wastewater is treated in an environmentally sound manner.*

6 It shall take precautions *to reduce waste and to recycle it. Non-recyclable waste shall be disposed of in an environmentally sound manner* or stored in a screened and accessible location.

7 The costs of disposal are borne by the producers of these goods through a price surcharge to be paid to the disposal companies.

8 The ministries of infrastructure, innovation and labour ensure a circular economy within the country's borders that does not require finite raw materials and is harmless to the animal and plant world. The Ministries of Economy cooperate with the Ministry of Innovation so that all companies of all economic forms can implement the requirements.

9 The Ministry of Integration, in cooperation with *private organisations, takes measures for the preservation of landscapes and sites worthy of protection, as well as natural monuments and cultural assets.*[344]

§191[345] Nature and homeland protection[346]

1 The Ministry of Infrastructure is responsible for *nature and homeland protection.*

2 In the fulfilment of its duties, it shall take into account the concerns of nature and homeland protection. It shall *protect landscapes, sites of local interest, historical sites and natural and cultural monuments and preserve them undiminished if the public interest so requires.*

3 It may *support efforts to protect nature and homeland protection and acquire or secure objects of* national *importance by treaty or by expropriation.* Compensation shall be paid in an appropriate

---

344 Ministry of Integration - 6 Integration
345 BV Art. 78
346 Ministry of Infrastructure - 4.1 Homeland protection, 4.2 Environmental protection

amount.

4 The Ministry of Health shall issue *regulations for the protection of fauna and flora and the preservation of their habitats in natural diversity.* It *protects endangered species from extinction.*[347]

5 Primeval natural areas of national *importance are protected. No installations may be built in them, nor may any changes be made to the soil. Excluded are* areas *that* lie within the Barter Economy Zone and may only be farmed with biodegradable items.[348]

§192[349] Water[350]

1 *Within the scope of its responsibilities,* the Ministry of Infrastructure shall ensure the economical *use and protection of water resources and the prevention of damage to water.*

2 It *lays down principles on the conservation and development of water resources, on the use of water bodies* as transport routes, *for energy production and for cooling purposes, and on other interventions in the water cycle.*

3 It shall *issue regulations on water protection, the securing of adequate residual flows, hydraulic engineering, the* construction and maintenance of *dams and the influencing of precipitation.*

4 *Water resources are at the disposal of the* municipalities. *They* levy *charges for the use of water within the limits of the law. They shall promote the economical and rational use of water.*

5 The Ministry of Infrastructure decides on rights to inter-municipal water *resources and associated charges with the involvement of the affected* municipalities. *If* municipalities *cannot agree on rights to* inter-municipal water resources, the national Ministry of Infrastructure shall decide.

6 The Ministry of Infrastructure takes into account *the concerns of the* municipalities from *which the water originates when carrying out its tasks.* It can force them to share water

---

347 Ministry of Health - 6.5 Sustainable use of nature, 6.5.2 Nature reserves
348 Ministry of Barter Economy - 6.1 Area, 9.4 Environmental Sustainability, 9.4.1 Inspection
349 BV Art. 76, KV Art.35
350 Ministry of Infrastructure - 4.9 Municipal Utilities Company, 4.9.1 Water Supply, 8.9 Navigation Network, 8.9.4 Flood Basins

with other municipalities. The sale of freshwater sources to foreigners and foreign companies is not permitted.

7 The Ministry of Health monitors the purity and health safety of tap water. It can order compulsory measures in the handling of water for other ministries and citizens in order to protect health.[351]

§193[352] Forest[353]

1 The ministries of labour, health and infrastructure ensure *that the forest can fulfil its protective, beneficial and welfare functions.*

2 They shall lay *down principles on the protection of the forest.*

3 They take measures to preserve *the forest.*

4 The Ministry of Barter Economy operates Barter Economy Zones in state forest areas. The life of the forest dwellers there must be environmentally neutral.

§194[354] Animal welfare[355]

1 The Ministry of Health shall issue *regulations on the protection of animals.*

2 *It regulates in particular:*

a. *the keeping and care of animals;*

b. *animal experiments and interventions on live animals;*

c. *the use of animals;*

d. *the import of animals and animal products;*

e. *the trade in and transport of animals;*

f. *the killing of* farm animals without causing stress to the animals.

3 *The Ministry of Health* is responsible for the enforcement of the regulations.

---

351 Ministry of Health - 4.4.3 Drinking water and forests
352 BV Art. 77
353 Ministry of Labour - 19.9 Forest, hunting and forestry policy, Ministry of Health - 4.4.3 Drinking water and forests, 6.5.2 Nature reserves, Ministry of Infrastructure - 4.2 Environmental protection, Ministry of Barter Economy - 6.1 Area
354 BV Art. 80
355 Ministry of Health - 6.5.3 Animal and Plant Protection

§195[356] Fishing and hunting[357]

The Ministry of Health lays down *principles on the practice of fishing and hunting, in particular for the conservation of biodiversity.*

§196[358] Spatial planning[359]

1 The Ministry of Infrastructure shall lay down *principles of spatial planning. These* serve the purposeful *and economical use of the land and the orderly settlement of the country.*
2 The nation shall promote, *coordinate and cooperate with* the *efforts of the* municipalities. The municipality shall obtain the following building regulations:
a. Municipalities ensure *the preservation of recreational space.*
b. *The spatial and building regulations shall be oriented towards the desired development* of the municipality. *It shall take into account the diverse needs of the population and the economy as well as the protection of the environment.*
c. The municipality shall ensure that sufficient *arable land is maintained.*
3 Foreigner influence in spatial planning is prohibited. Land and real estate located on the site within the inland boundary but owned by foreigners may be expropriated. Adequate financial compensation shall be provided.
4 The sale of land within the country to foreigners is not permitted. Only renting or leasing is permitted. The Ministry of Integration shall determine further details in the law.

---

356 BV Art. 79
357 Ministry of Health - 6.5.5 Agriculture
358 BV Art. 75, KV Art.33
359 Ministry of Foreign Affairs - 7.3.11 International Economic Policy, Ministry of Infrastructure - 4 Homeland, Ministry of Integration - 7.2 Residence

§197[360] **Surveying**[361]

1 Land surveying is the responsibility of the Ministry of Infrastructure.
2 It shall *issue regulations on official cadastral surveying.*
3 It *may, in voting with* the Ministry of Digital Affairs, issue *regulations on the harmonisation of official information concerning land.*
4 It reports its findings to the Ministry of Digital Affairs.

§198[362] **Home ownership**[363]

1 The Ministry of Infrastructure <u>operates state housing</u> until 95% of the nationals own their own homes.
2 The share of secondary residences in the total number of residential units and the floor area used *for residential purposes in a* municipality *is limited to a maximum of 20 percent.*
3 The Ministry of Infrastructure determines the appropriate restriction through the municipal and national home ownership rate.
4 Second homes may be allocated without limit if the municipal home ownership rate is at least 95%.

Chapter 6: State enterprises and Transport

§199 **State enterprises**[364]

1 All ministries may establish and operate state enterprises to provide services to citizens. The Ministry of Labour ensures entrepreneurially efficient operations and regularly audits

---

360 BV Art. 75a
361 Ministry of Digital Affairs - 6 Statistical Office, Ministry of Infrastructure - 4 Homeland, 4.3.1 Institute of Earth Sciences and Natural Resources
362 KV Art.40, BV Art. 75b
363 Ministry of Infrastructure - 4.4.2 Home ownership rate, 5.13 Housebuilding programme
364 Ministry of Labour - 4 State enterprises, Ministry of Innovation - 10 People's Innovation Company, Ministry of Infrastructure - 4.9 Municipal Utilities Company, 4.9.2 Waste disposal, 5 Building, 9.7 Energy Supply, 9.7.2 Central

compliance with the requirements. The state enterprises are to generate a maximum of 10% profits, which they pay into the state budget for the coming year. The Ministry of Labour determines the details in the law.

2 The Ministry of Innovation operates People's Innovation Companies. People's Innovation Companies base their companies on patented products and processes. Until the expiry date of the patent protection, monopoly profits are to be generated, which replace tax money. The Ministry of Innovation determines the details in the law.

3 The Ministry of Infrastructure builds all state enterprises and People's Innovation Companies in voting with the responsible ministries. It builds and operates the state enterprises for energy, waste disposal, water and waste water. It builds and operates:

a. Pumped-storage power stations along water pipelines and watercourses stretching from the sea coast to the high mountains;

b. Energy generation systems for wave power, tidal range, current, wind power and solar energy.

§200[365] Traffic[366]

1 The Ministry of Infrastructure ensures the development of all areas of the country.

2 It shall ensure *a sufficient supply of* modern transport infrastructure on land, at *sea, in the* air, in space *and with cableways in all regions of the country.* It shall levy a cost-covering charge on users for this purpose.

3 Freight traffic shall be transported on land by rail until onward rail transport to the customer is no longer possible.

4 The Ministry of Infrastructure is constantly innovating in the transport sector to avoid the fragmentation of the landscape by roads and railways. The medium-term goal is to shift motorised transport for goods underground and human motorised transport to the air.

---

365 BV Art. 81a
366 Ministry of Infrastructure - 6 Networks, 8 Traffic, 8.7.6 Financing of the road network, 8.8.5 Financing of the rail network

5 The costs of the state transport companies and the transport infrastructure for private and commercial use *are (...) covered by the prices paid by the users.* The prices cover in particular all measures for maintenance and environmental protection. The prices shall be based on the means of transport and on the effort required to provide the necessary infrastructure and to repair or prevent any damage caused.

§201[367] Road traffic[368]

1 The Ministry of Infrastructure *issues* laws on *road transport.*
2 It shall *exercise overall supervision over the roads (...). It may determine which thoroughfares must remain open to traffic.*
3 It builds, *operates and maintains the* roads.
4 It ensures *safe, economical, environmentally sound and energy-saving traffic regulations.*
5 It operates state transport and promotes *the switch to environmentally friendly modes of transport.*
6 It takes into account the *needs of non-motorised traffic when building roads.*
7 It takes into account the *impact on traffic volumes when performing its tasks.*
8 *The use* of state *roads is free of charge* for pedestrians and cyclists. The Ministry of Infrastructure levies a regular charge on motorised vehicles weighing 100 kilograms or more. The rates are to be adjusted to the degree of use of roads and the environment by the vehicle.

§202[369] Transit traffic[370]

1 The Ministry of Infrastructure *protects the national* territory from *the negative effects of transit traffic.* It shall *limit the pollution caused by transit traffic to a level that is not harmful to humans, animals and plants and their habitats.*
2 The (...) transit of goods from border to border shall take place

---

367 BV Art. 82, 83, KV Art.34
368 Ministry of Infrastructure - 8 Traffic, 8.7 Road network, 8.7.3 Public transport, 8.7.6 Road network financing, 8.8.5 Rail network financing.
369 BV Art. 84
370 Ministry of Infrastructure - 8 Traffic

by rail. (...) Exceptions are only permitted if they are unavoidable. They must be specified in more detail by a law.

§203[371] Heavy Vehicle Fee[372]

1 The Ministry of Infrastructure may levy a charge on heavy goods traffic based on performance *or consumption insofar as heavy goods traffic causes* additional *costs to the general public that are not covered by other services or charges.*
2 The net proceeds of the charge shall be used to cover costs associated with heavy goods vehicles.

§204[373] Footpaths and hiking trails[374]

1 The Ministry of Infrastructure establishes *principles on* cycling, walking and hiking *trail networks.*
2 It shall take *measures (...) to establish and maintain such networks.*
3 It shall, in the *performance of its duties, take account of* cycle, *footpath and footpath networks and replace paths which* it is *required to abandon.*

Chapter 7: Energy and Communication

§205[375] Energy policy[376]

1 The Ministry of Infrastructure shall, within the *scope of* its responsibilities, promote an adequate, *diversified, secure, economic and environmentally sound energy supply and the economical and rational use of energy.*

---

371 BV Art. 85
372 Ministry of Infrastructure - 8.7.6 Financing of the road network, 8.8.5 Financing of the rail network
373 BV Art. 88
374 Ministry of Infrastructure - 8.7 Road network
375 BV Art. 89
376 Ministry of Infrastructure - 5 Construction, 9 Energy, 9.5 Energy transition, 9.7.1 Decentralised, 9.7.2 Centralised, 9.8 New power development

2 It shall lay down *principles on the use of domestic and renewable energies and on the economical and rational consumption of energy.*

3 It shall issue *regulations on the energy consumption of installations, vehicles and devices.* It shall *promote the development of energy technologies, in particular in the areas of energy saving and renewable energies.*

4 The municipal employees of the Ministry of Infrastructure *are responsible for measures concerning the consumption of energy in buildings.*

5 The Ministry of Infrastructure takes into account the conditions *in the individual areas of the country and the economic viability.*

6 The generation of energy from geothermal heat, nuclear fission and coal is only permitted until the renewable energy system can cover 120% of the country's energy needs. The costs for this expansion of renewable energy will be covered by the profit revenues from geothermal energy, nuclear fission and coal. The dismantling of obsolete energy sources is financed from profit revenues from renewable energies.

§206[377] Transport of energy, data, water and waste water[378]

1 The Ministry of Infrastructure shall issue *regulations on the transport and supply of electrical energy* and liquid or gaseous *fuels*, data, water and waste water.

2 It operates renewable energy transport facilities capable of adequately supporting the country with electricity, data, energy, water and wastewater.

3 It shall ensure the construction of the installations, networks and lines and their maintenance.

---

377 BV Art. 91
378 Ministry of Infrastructure - 5 Construction, 6 Networks

§207[379] Telecommunications[380]

1 Telecommunications (...) is the responsibility of the Ministry of Digital Affairs.

2 It shall *ensure an adequate and inexpensive basic supply of (...) telecommunications services in all areas of the country. Tariffs shall be set according to uniform principles of* cost recovery.

3 It protects citizens' data and ensures the prevention of criminal offences in digital networks.

4 It operates an intranet in which citizens can administer their private and business relations and together as a people the state in a direct democratic manner. It creates the necessary directories, programmes and devices.

5 It supports citizens with transmitting and receiving devices for the intranet at cost price. Production takes place in Planned Economy factories and in the security sector of the Ministry of Digital Affairs.

6 The intranet serves all domestic nationals and politicians for direct democratic participation, use of the people's swarm intelligence, forecasting of the future and digital and transparent collection and storage of data.

7 The Ministry of Digital Affairs guarantees the security and authenticity of all data, treaties and votes on the intranet.

§208[381] State media[382]

1 The Ministry of Media Affairs operates state radio stations. The broadcasters are separated according to their tasks.

a. A broadcaster shall provide for the presentation of negotiations by politicians on state treaties, instructions or laws and shall enable those entitled to vote to participate digitally in the negotiations, especially for voting purposes.

b. A broadcaster shall ensure the presentation of all activities

---

379 BV Art. 92

380 Ministry of Digital Affairs - 3 Tasks of the Ministry of Digital Affairs, 7 Digital data protection, 11 Intranet, 13 People's Innovation Company Intranet, 14 Programmes, 15.3 Algoracle

381 BV Art. 93

382 Ministry of Media Affairs - 5 State broadcasting, 5.1 Broadcasting operations

of all ministries in cooperation with those ministries.

c. A broadcaster shall ensure the presentation of unannounced controls on all activities of all ministries.

d. A broadcaster shall ensure the presentation of all educational content necessary to complete degrees at state schools and colleges.

e. One broadcaster ensures the presentation of content from the other broadcasters in child-friendly expression.

2 All broadcasters operate pages on the intranet where citizens can rate the broadcasters' staff and content. The ratings result in a new election of staff or a change of content in case of a majority of affected citizens.

3 All broadcasters contribute to education, *state* direction and control, and the *free formation of opinion (...). They take into account the special features of the country and the needs of the* municipalities. *They present events in a factual manner and adequately express the diversity of views of* all constituents.

§209[383] Press[384]

1 Legislation on freedom of the press in *radio and television and on other forms of* non-state dissemination *of performances and information is the responsibility of the Ministry of Media Affairs.*

2 The free media shall contribute to education *and cultural development, to the free formation of opinion and to entertainment. (...) They present events in a factual manner and adequately express the diversity of views.*

3 The independence of the press *as well as the autonomy in programming are guaranteed.*

4 Equal *consideration shall be given to the position and mission of other* non-state media.

5 Programme complaints may be submitted to an independent complaints body.

---

383 BV Art. 93

384 Ministry of Media Affairs - 4.1 Freedom of the Press

Chapter 8: Economy

§210[385] Principles of economic order[386]

1 The Ministries of Labour, Barter Economy, Planned Economy, Social Market Economy and Free Market Economy *adhere to the principle of economic freedom.* This includes, in particular, freedom of choice and mobility between the four economic forms.

2 They safeguard the interests of the domestic economy *and contribute to the welfare and economic security of the population with* the four economic forms. They *create favourable framework conditions for a structurally and regionally balanced, productive economy.*

3 The Ministry of Social Market Economy strives *to maintain viable small and medium enterprises and a broad-based* retail sector.

4 Deviations from the principle of economic freedom, (...) are only permissible if fair *competition* is violated in the form of price fixing, the creation of information asymmetries between buyers and sellers or the creation of external effects by shifting costs to the environment or third parties. The Ministry of Labour shall determine further details in the law.

5 Other deviations from the principle of economic freedom are possible in the Barter Economy, Planned Economy and Social Market Economy and must be enacted by law by the responsible ministries.

6 State property may only be sold or privatised after a referendum.

7 The country's mineral resources belong to the people as a whole. The country's mineral resources may only be exploited by state enterprises. Any profits made from this are to be regarded as the people's property and are to be included in the

---

385BV Art. 94, KV Art.50

386Ministry of Labour - 9 Principles of Hybrid Economic Systems, 15 Antitrust Agency, 19.7 Mineral Resources, 20.7.3 Economic Auditor, 20.7.3.1 State Audit, 20.7.6.2 Constitutional Law Audit, Ministry of Free Market Economy - 4 Economic Policy, Ministry of Social Market Economy - 4 Economic Policy, Ministry of Planned Economy - 9 Basic Supply Work Area, 10 Luxury Supply Work Area, Ministry of Barter Economy - 4 Economic Policy

budget vote for the following year.

8 The Ministry of Labour checks whether the companies and employees of all enterprises comply with the regulations of their economic form.

§211[387] National supply[388]

1 The Ministry of Security shall ensure the supply of essential assets *and services to the country in the event of political or military threats, as well as in the event of severe shortages that the economy is unable to address itself. It takes precautionary measures.*

2 It *may derogate from the principle of economic freedom* for disaster management.

3 The state is always in a position to support all nationals with all essential goods on a permanent basis in case of emergency. To this end, it maintains a stockpile and makes appropriate provisions through its ministries.

4 The ministries of Barter Economy, Planned Economy and Social Market Economy support the domestic population with food, clothing, building materials, data, electricity and water in the event of a disaster. For this purpose, an emergency plan is to convert the current operation. The Ministry of Security determines the details of the emergency plan in the law.

§212[389] Structural policy[390]

1 The Ministry of Labour may support *economically structurally* weak areas of the country and *promote economic sectors and professions if reasonable self-help measures are not sufficient to secure their existence.*

387BV Art. 102

388Ministry of Security - 5.7 Disaster management, Ministry of Social Market Economy - 18 Disaster management, Ministry of Planned Economy - 20 Disaster management, Ministry of Barter Economy - 17 Disaster management

389BV Art. 103

390Ministry of Labour - 9.5 Structural support, 20.7.7 Business consultants, Ministry of Innovation - 6.5 Mobile Innovation Labs, 10.3 Construction projects, Ministry of Digital Affairs - 6 Statistical Office

2 It *may, if necessary, deviate from the principle of economic freedom.*

3 It provides credit-financed economic advice through the Company Auditing Agency to all domestic companies in structurally weak areas of the country, which only has to be repaid if the proposed measures are successful.

4 The Ministry of Innovation builds People's Innovation Companies in structurally weak areas of the country that apply for them.

5 It sends mobile Innovation Labs especially to structurally weak areas.

6 The Ministry of Labour, in voting with the Ministry of Digital Affairs, determines which areas are structurally weak.

§213[391] Economic policy[392]

1 The Ministry of Finance shall take *measures for a balanced economic development, in particular to prevent and combat unemployment and inflation.*

2 It takes into account *the economic development of the individual regions of the country* and works *together with the ministries of* economy.

3 In the monetary and credit system, in foreign trade and in the area of state *finances,* it may, *if necessary, deviate from the principle of economic freedom.* Deviations shall require the consent of the people.

4 All ministries take *the economic situation into account in their revenues and expenditure policies.*

5 The Ministry of Finance may temporarily impose *surcharges* on taxes to *stabilise the economy* in an upswing phase. *The surcharged funds shall be set aside. After release* during a downturn phase, the funds shall be granted as *rebates* on taxes to the same extent.

6 The Ministry of Finance *may require companies* and ministries to build *up* asset reserves. *Companies are allowed to use* the *reserves* as soon as they suffer losses. Ministries may use them

---

391 BV Art. 100

392 Ministry of Finance - 7.5 Balancing the business cycles, 8.4 Profits, 9.1 Financial plans of the ministries

if they would violate the requirements of the budget vote.

§214[393] Competition policy[394]

1 The Ministry of Labour shall, in voting with the ministries of economy, *issue regulations against economically or socially harmful effects of cartels and other restrictions of competition.*
2 It takes *measures:*
a. to prevent abuses in pricing by companies and organisations under private and state law with market power.
b. against unfair competition.
3 It also uses undercover investigations, test purchases and unannounced investigations to fulfil the measures.

§215[395] Gainful employment[396]

1 The Ministry of Labour may issue *regulations on the exercise of (…) gainful employment* which shall apply to all economic forms.
2 It ensures *a uniform* domestic *economic area.* It *ensures that persons with a degree from* a domestic educational institution *can practise their profession throughout* the country.
3 It shall ensure a smooth and lawful transition of capital and labour between economic forms. It shall issue regulations for this purpose in voting with the four ministries of economy.
4 It ensures that unemployed people get the training they want and that unemployed domestic nationals in the Planned Economy always get a job.
5 It ensures that occupational health and safety regulations apply to all workers.
6 It regularly audits the companies in a survey. It asks employees anonymously about their working conditions and suggestions

---

393 BV Art. 96
394 Ministry of Labour - 15 Antitrust Agency
395 BV Art. 95
396 Ministry of Labour - 10.1 Enterprises in several economic forms, 10.2 Switching between economic forms, 11.2 Vocational training, 11.2.1 Necessary training content, 12.2.1 Employment exchange, 14.2 Occupational safety and health, 20 Company Auditing Agency, 20.7.1.1 Tax auditing of companies

for improvement. It checks compliance with the regulations of the respective economic form. It checks the tax payments made. It checks the economic efficiency of the companies and reports discovered deficiencies to the company.

§216[397] Joint-stock companies[398]

1 For the *protection of the national economy, private property and shareholders, as well as for the purpose of sustainable corporate governance,* each *Ministry of Economy shall regulate domestic joint-stock companies* listed at *home or abroad in accordance with the following principles:*

a. The General Meeting of all shareholders and employees shall vote annually *on the total amount of all compensation (cash and value in kind) of the Board of Directors, the Executive Board and the Advisory Board. It shall elect annually the Chairman of the Board of Directors and individually the members of the Board of Directors and the Compensation Committee as well as the independent proxy. The pension funds vote in the interest of their members and disclose how they voted. Shareholders* and employees *may vote remotely by electronic means. Proxy voting by governing bodies and custody accounts is prohibited.*

b. The members of the governing bodies shall not receive any severance or other compensation, any remuneration in advance, any premium for company acquisitions and sales and any additional consultancy or employment contract from another company of the Group. The management of the Company cannot be delegated to a legal person.

c. The Articles of Association shall regularise the amount of loans, credits and pensions granted to the members of the governing bodies, their performance and shareholding plans and the number of mandates they hold outside the corporation, as well as the duration of the employment contracts of the members of the

---

397 BV Art. 95
398 Ministry of Labour - 18.2 Joint-stock companies, Ministry of Free Market Economy - 10.3 Stock exchanges, Ministry of Social Market Economy - 13.4 Joint-stock companies, Ministry of Planned Economy - 13.4 Planned Economy joint-stock companies, Ministry of Barter Economy - 9 Enterprise policy

Executive Board.
d. Violation of *the provisions under letters a to c shall be punishable by imprisonment for a term of up to three years and a fine of up to six annual salaries.*
2 Joint-stock companies are prohibited in the Barter Economy.
3 In Planned Economy, only employees of the Planned Economy joint-stock company may be shareholders of that joint-stock company.
4 In the Social Market Economy, only domestic citizens living inland may be shareholders in a social economy joint-stock company.
5 Dividends must be paid duty on by the joint-stock companies at the VAT rate if they are paid into a foreign account.

§217[399] Banks and insurance companies[400]

1 The ministries of economy shall issue *regulations on banking and stock exchange for their respective economic forms. In doing so,* they shall take into *account the special task and position of the domestic Central Bank* as the guardian of all currencies.
2 They may *issue regulations on financial services.*
3 They shall issue *regulations on* insurance.
4 The Ministry of Labour verifies compliance.

§218[401] State bank[402]

1 The Ministry of Finance establishes the People's Bank as the national state bank.
2 The head of the People's Bank is an elected politician.
3 The People's Bank promotes *economic and social development.* *It helps* the nation, municipalities and citizens lend money to

---

399 BV Art. 98
400 Ministry of Labour - 18.3 Financial Supervisory Authority, 20.7.3.2 Private Sector Audit, Ministry of Free Market Economy - 10.2 Banks, 10.3 Stock Exchanges, Ministry of Social Market Economy - 13.2 Banking Regulations, 13.2 People's Stock Exchange, 17.5 Compulsory Insurance, Ministry of Planned Economy - 13 Finance Economy, Ministry of Barter Economy - 12.2 Banks, 12.3 Insurance.
401 KV Art.53
402 Ministry of Finance - 11 People's Bank

each other for companies. The Ministry of Labour audits the companies through its Company Auditing Agency.

4 The People's Bank is prohibited from doing business with foreigners. Exceptions must be made by law through the Ministry of Finance and require the consent of the people. Loans may only be granted to domestic nationals for business purposes. Lending for consumption purposes is reserved for banks in the free market economy.

5 The People's Bank is the only bank in whose account all currencies of all economic forms can be deposited. It ensures the equitable transfer of monetary assets between economic forms. It is not allowed to hand over this business to other banks.

6 Citizens living in the Barter Economy and Planned Economy are only allowed to have one bank account with the People's Bank to invest their financial assets.[403]

7 The People's Bank is the only bank where all ministries are allowed to keep their bank accounts and which also holds the state budget. Citizens can lend to the state and domestic companies through their bank accounts at People's Bank.

8 The state cooperates with voluntary domestic nationals through the People's Bank to jointly finance the state budget.

§219[404] Central Bank and currency policy[405]

1 The Ministry of Finance is responsible for monetary affairs. It establishes a Central Bank and four Note-issuing Banks, which *alone have the right to issue coins and banknotes.*

---

403 Planned Economy - 6.3.2 Financial Move, 13.3 Financial Services, Ministry of Barter Economy -12.2 Banks
404 BV Art. 99
405 Ministry of Finance - 10 Central Bank, 10.2.1 Price stability and full employment, 10.3.3 Exchange rates, 10.3.5 Foreign reserves, 10.4 Note-issuing Banks, 10.4.1 Objectives of Note-issuing Banks, 10.4.2.1 Key issue rate, 10.4.2.2 Key deposit rate, Ministry of Labour - 10.2 Switching between economic forms, Ministry of Free Market Economy - 10.1 Currency, Ministry of Social Market Economy - 13.1 National currency of Social Market Economy, Ministry of Planned Economy - 7.6.2 Working hours account, 8.3 Working hours account, 13.1 Currency policy, 13.2 Digital currency Working hours, Ministry of Barter Economy - 12.1 Currency, 12.2 Banks, 12.3 Insurances

Supranational currencies may be issued by the Central Bank of an International Union in which the inland is in voting with other countries.

2 The Central Bank shall *(...) conduct a monetary and currency policy which serves the overall economic interest of the country.* Each Note-issuing Bank shall conduct a monetary and currency policy which serves the national economic interest of its economic form. The head of the Central Bank and Note-issuing Banks shall be elected politicians.

3 Note-issuing Banks administer all currencies of the economic forms:

a. The Barter Economy uses goods and services as currency.

b. The Planned Economy has a digital currency in labour per hour.

c. The Social Market Economy uses a national currency.

d. The Free Market Economy uses a supranational currency.

4 The Central Bank, in voting with the Note-issuing Banks, determines the exchange rates of the tradable currencies in the country.

5 The Ministry of Labour determines laws for switching capital and labour between economic forms.

6 The Central Bank is committed to the economic goals of price stability and full employment.

7 It builds up sufficient *currency reserves from* the *earnings of* the Note-issuing Banks. *Part of these reserves is held in gold,* other parts in scarce, non-perishable or difficult-to-perish commodities.

8 *The net profit of the Note-issuing Banks* through interest rate transactions ensures an economically efficient and fair balance between the economic forms. It is expelled as an available amount in the annual budget vote.

§220[406] Agriculture[407]

1 The *Ministry of Labour shall ensure that agriculture,* in all *economic forms, makes a significant contribution to the development of the economy through sustainable production*

406BV Art. 104, KV Art.51, BV Art. 197

407Ministry of Labour - 19 Agriculture, Ministry of Education -

geared to the domestic market:
a. safe supply of the population;
b. Conservation of natural resources and care of the landscape through the Social Market Economy and Planned Economy;
c. productive *and environmentally sound agriculture and forestry* through the Free Market Economy and Barter Economy;
d. Supporting *family farmers* through purchasing and use cooperatives of modern inputs in the Social Market Economy and Planned Economy;
e. Promote *near-natural management practices* through research and exchange forums for successful strategies;
f. Safeguarding and *preserving the forests in their protective, useful and welfare functions.*
2 It shall, in addition to reasonable *self-help,* promote agriculture *and, if necessary, in derogation of the principle of economic freedom, promote farming companies* in the Barter Economy, Planned Economy and Social Market Economy.
3 It shall *direct the measures so that agriculture fulfils its multifunctional tasks. In particular, it shall have the following powers and tasks:*
a. It provides crop failure insurance and *supplements farmers' income through direct payments in case of crop failure due to drought,* storms, fire or floods. The Ministry of Infrastructure is responsible for precautions against droughts and floods through water pipes and catchment tanks.
b. It provides direct services *to earn an appropriate fee for the services provided, subject to an environmental performance record* with the Company Auditing Agency.
c. It shall promote *(...) forms of production that are particularly close to nature, environmentally friendly and animal-friendly* through export permits to other economic forms or countries.
d. It shall, in voting with the Ministry of Health, *issue regulations on the* labelling *of the origin, quality, production*

9.15.2.9 Biology, 9.15.2.10 Geography, 9.15.2.12 Crafts, Ministry of Health - 6.3 Food safety, 6.5 Sustainable use of nature, 6.5.5 Agriculture, 6.5.6 Genetic engineering, Ministry of Infrastructure - 4 Homeland, Ministry of Innovation - 5.4.1 Provision for the future, Ministry of Free Market Economy - 11 Agriculture, Ministry of Social Market Economy - 14 Agriculture, 14.3 Agricultural cooperative, 14.4 Harvesters, Ministry of Planned Economy - 11.1.10 Mineral resources, 14.5 Market garden, 18.1.5 Energy centre, Ministry of Barter Economy - 13 Agriculture

method and processing methods of foodstuffs.
e. It shall, in voting with the Ministry of Health, *protect the environment from degradation caused by* the *use of medicines,* fertilisers, *chemicals,* genetic modification *and other adjuvants.*
f. The Ministry of Education promotes agricultural research, *advice and training.*
g. The Ministry of Innovation can provide *investment aid* if new technology helps to achieve higher yields while maintaining or improving nature, environmental and animal protection.
h. The Ministry of Infrastructure may issue *regulations to consolidate peasant land ownership.* The sale or lease of agricultural land to foreigners is prohibited until domestic demand is met.
4 The Ministry of Health supervises the use of genetic engineering in agriculture and prevents any contact of genetically engineered products with the environment during the production process. In particular, *genetically* modified *seeds,* pollen, *plants* and *animals* must not enter the free ecosystem.
5 The Ministry of Planned Economy administers the country's mineral resources in voting with the people. Namely, these are the reserves of groundwater and mineral resources below and above ground within the country's and sea borders. The exclusive right of exploitation can be transferred to municipalities.

§221[408] Drugs[409]

1 Legislation on the production, import, purity and sale of drugs of all kinds is the responsibility of the Ministry of Health.
2 It issues purity laws for all drugs.
3 It *takes particular account of the harmful effects of* drug use. It operates its own Addictive Drugs Health Insurance for this purpose. The contributions to this health insurance come from price surcharges on addictive drugs. The amount of the contribution is based on the harmfulness and addictiveness of the substance or activity consumed.

---

408 BV Art. 105
409 Ministry of Health - 5.11 Drugs, 5.11.2 Purity Law, 5.12.3 Addictive drugs Health Insurance

§222[410] Money games[411]

1 The Ministry of Labour shall issue *regulations on money games*. It shall coordinate the regulations with the Ministry of Health.

2 The Company Auditing Agency of the Ministry of Labour monitors compliance.

3 A licence from the Ministry of Labour *is required for the establishment and operation of casinos* and gaming machines. (...) It *levies a revenue-based casino tax. This may not exceed 80 percent of the gross gaming revenue. This levy is earmarked for the* Addictive drugs Health Insurance.

4 The *Ministry of Labour* is *responsible for authorisation and supervision:*

a. of money games open to an unlimited number of persons, offered in multiple locations or digitally, *and subject to* a random draw *or similar procedure.*

b. sports betting;

c. financial market betting;

d. *the games of skill.*

5 *Paragraphs 2, 3* and 4 shall *also apply to cash games conducted* digitally.

6 The Ministry of Health shall take into account *the dangers of gambling*. It shall *ensure adequate protection through legislation and supervisory measures,* taking into account the *different characteristics of the games as well as the type and location of the gambling offer.*

§223[412] Weapons and war material[413]

1 The Ministry of Security shall issue *regulations against the* private possession of lethal *weapons, weapon accessories and ammunition.*

2 It shall *issue regulations on the* prohibition of the private

---

410 BV Art. 106

411 Ministry of Health - 4.4.2 Health risks, 5.12.3 Addictive drugs Health Insurance, Ministry of Labour - 18.1 Money games, 18.3 Financial Supervisory Authority

412 BV Art. 107

413 Ministry of Security - 4.7 Weapons legislation

manufacture, procurement, private *distribution and the import, export and transit of* lethal weapons and *war material.*[414]
3 Owners of lethal weapons used in shooting clubs or for hunting purposes shall deposit their weapons at the local police station outside the periods of use.
4 Weapons production for the services of the Ministry of Security is handled by the Ministry of Planned Economy.[415]
5 The Ministry of Security ensures that citizens are armed in case of war.
6 The Ministry of Security refrains from using lethal weapons in the police service. This excludes special operations to fight enemies who use lethal weapons or directly threaten the lives of others.

§224[416] Protection of consumers[417]

1 The Ministry of Labour takes measures to protect *consumers.*
2 It shall *issue regulations on the legal remedies that consumer organisations may take. These organisations shall have the same rights in the area of* legislation *on unfair competition as professional and trade associations.*
3 The Ministry of Labour shall provide for municipal conciliation *or simple and speedy court proceedings for disputes up to a certain amount in dispute.* It shall *determine the limit of the amount in dispute.*

§225[418] Foreign trade policy[419]

1 The Ministry of Labour, in voting with the Ministries of Economy and Foreign Affairs, shall *safeguard the interests of the* domestic *economy abroad.*

---

414 Ministry of Foreign Affairs - 5.4 Free Trade Agreements, 7.2.10 Arms Control
415 Ministry of Planned Economy - 10.5.2 State orders
416 BV Art. 97
417 Ministry of Labour - 17 Consumer protection
418 BV Art. 101
419 Ministry of Finance - 11.3 Foreign trade, Ministry of Labour - 10.3.1 Restrictions, Ministry of Foreign Affairs - 6.4.2.4.3 Planned Economy, 6.4.2.4 Barter Economy, 7.2.10 Arms control, 7.3.11 International

2 In special cases, it may take *measures to protect the domestic economy. If necessary,* it *may deviate from the principle of economic freedom.*

3 The Barter Economy is not authorised to engage in foreign trade.

4 The Planned Economy is not eligible for foreign trade unless domestic demand is saturated or the exporters are Experimental Enterprises, Innovation Enterprises or People's Innovation Companies.

5 The export of weapons of war and state-subsidised goods and services is prohibited.

6 The people have the right to prohibit the export of weapons or food for a limited or unlimited period by a quorum of 40%.

7 Other foreign trade of goods, services and companies must be negotiated in trade contracts. The Ministries of Labour, Foreign Affairs and Finance, the Ministry of Economy of the economic form affected and the people must be involved in the contract negotiations.

8 The sale of domestic land and housing to international corporations or companies is prohibited. Only nationals own the land that their state governs. Foreigners can only rent land.

9 The state is prohibited from borrowing abroad; only domestic nationals may lend money to their state.

Chapter 9: Housing, Work, Social Security & Health

§226[420] Housing and home ownership promotion[421]

1 The Ministry of Infrastructure *promotes housing construction, the acquisition of housing and home ownership for the own use* of domestic nationals. *It operates non-profit housing construction*

---

economic policy, 7.3.13 International financial policy, Ministry of
Free Market Economy - 12 Foreign trade, Ministry of Social Market
Economy - 15 Foreign trade, Ministry of Planned Economy - 15 Foreign
trade, Ministry of Barter Economy - 14 Foreign trade
420 BV Art. 108, KV Art.40
421 Ministry of Education - 9.15.1.7 Eleventh learning year subject:
housebuilding, 9.15.2.12 Crafts, Ministry of Infrastructure - 5 Building,
5.1 Building Office, 5.4 Building permits, 5.10 Infrastructurators, 5.12
Building materials, 5.13 Housebuilding programme, Ministry of Planned

in cooperation with residents of the planned economy and learners from educational institutions.

2 It shall in *particular promote the procurement and development of land for housing construction, the rationalisation and cheapening of housing construction and the cheapening of housing costs.*

3 It *may make regulations on the development of land for housing,* areas of exchange or planned economy *and construction rationalisation.*

4 It shall *take particular account of the interests of families, the elderly, the needy and the disabled.*

5 It ensures a high rate of home ownership among citizens with the help of the housebuilding programme.

6 It takes <u>*measures for the preservation of affordable housing and for the improvement of inadequate housing conditions*</u>. It promotes low-cost housing <u>*construction*</u> through state enterprises that produce ready-made construction modules and multifunctional construction machinery.

§227[422] **Rental business**[423]

1 The Ministry of Economy, which is responsible for real estate, shall issue *regulations against abuses in the rental sector, namely against abusive rents, as well as on the contestability of abusive terminations and the temporary extension of tenancies.*

2 It *may issue regulations on the declaration of general applicability of framework tenancy agreements. Such agreements may only be declared generally binding if they take due account of justified minority interests and regional differences and do not impair equality of rights.*

3 Landlords must register their rental activity as a company with their chosen Ministry of Economy.

Economy - 9.4.5.1 Caretaker, Ministry of Barter Economy - 11 Real estate sector

422 BV Art. 109

423 Ministry of Free Market Economy - 9 Real estate sector, Ministry of Social Market Economy - 12, 12.2.1 Leases, 12.2.2 Rent control, Ministry of Planned Economy - 5.7.1 Economic fluctuations, 6.3.2 Financial move, 12.2 Tenancy, Ministry of Barter Economy - 11.3 Tenants and landlords

§228[424] **Labour**[425]

1 The Ministry *of Labour may,* after voting *with the responsible Ministry* or *Ministries of Economy, issue regulations on:*
a. the protection of workers;
b. the relationship between the employer and the employees, in particular on the joint regularisation of company and professional matters;
c. the employment exchange;
d. the declaration of general applicability of collective agreements.
2 Collective agreements may only be declared generally binding if they take due account of justified minority interests and regional differences and do not impair equality of rights and freedom of association.
3 The seventh of July is a bank holiday. *It is equal to Sundays in terms of labour law and is paid.*
4 All labourers must rest their labour activity one day per week.
5 The Ministry of Labour *promotes occupational safety and occupational health.*
6 It does not take part in *lawful industrial action between social partners and does not take sides.* Exceptions are determined by affected ministries of economy in voting with the Ministry of Labour in the law.
7 It promotes the *compatibility of gainful employment and care responsibilities.*
8 It takes precautions *to prevent unemployment and to mitigate its consequences.* It supports vocational retraining *and reintegration.* The Ministry of Planned Economy provides housing and employment for unemployed domestic nationals.

---

424 BV Art. 110, KV Art.39
425 Ministry of Labour - 9.3 Laws and taxes for companies, Passive labour market promotion, 14.1 Public holidays, 14.2 Occupational safety and health, 16 Employee protection, 16.4 Partner work, 16.7 Industrial action, 20.7.2.1 Occupational health and safety audit, Ministry of Free Market Economy - 6 Enterprise policy, Ministry of Social Market Economy - 8 Collective labour agreements, Ministry of Planned Economy - 7 Enterprise policy, 7.2 Occupational health and safety for all work areas, 18.2.7 External in-service training, 18.3 Employment exchange, Ministry of Barter Economy - 9 Enterprise policy

§229[426] Unemployment, old-age, survivors' and disability pensions[427]

1 The Ministry of Labour *takes measures to ensure adequate* unemployment, *old-age,* survivors' *and* disability benefits. *This is based on three pillars, namely* permanent access to the planned economy as social insurance for all domestics, occupational pension provision *and self-provision.*
2 The Ministry of Planned Economy shall *ensure that* domestic unemployment, *old-age,* survivors' *and* disability benefits *can fulfil their purpose on a permanent basis.*
3 It *may,* after voting with the people or affected citizens, oblige municipalities *to be converted* into a Planned Economy area.
4 It *promotes* citizen-initiated honorary service in and between municipalities for *self-provisioning namely by lending out state* assets or real estate.

§230[428] Social security[429]

1 The Ministry of Planned Economy shall *issue regulations on* social security.
2 It shall *observe the following principles:*
a. Planned Economy is open to all domestic nationals at all times.
b. The working plan is created by all participants of Planned Economy in a direct democratic way in the needs assessment and in the duty roster.
c. The Ministry of Planned Economy *provides (...) benefits in kind* for adequate *subsistence needs.* Cash benefits shall be paid

---

426 BV Art. 111
427 Ministry of Labour - 12.1.2 Provision, Ministry of Planned Economy - 4.8 Activity communities, 5 Economic policy, 5.2 Regional economic policy, 5.8 New construction of a Social Village, 6.1 Entrance into Planned Economy, 6.1.2 Moving in necessarily, 18.1.6 House for disabled people.
428 BV Art. 112
429 Ministry of Planned Economy - 6.1 Entrance to Planned Economy, 6.1.2.5 Pension, 7.6 Duty roster, 9 Work area Basic supply, 10.8 Experimental Enterprises, 10.8.2 Start-up Fund, 16.3 Financing of social welfare

in the digital currency of the Planned Economy, which can only be used for payment in the Planned Economy.

d. The uniform pensions of the Planned Economy *shall adequately cover the subsistence needs. The pensions shall be (...) adjusted to the price development* of the economic form in which they were earned.

e. Start-ups are promoted so that new companies with former unemployed as employees can participate in the markets of other economic forms. For this purpose, a Start-up Fund is set up from which start-ups are financed. Companies whose start-ups are financed by the fund pay 3% of their profits into the fund each year.

3 Social security *is financed:*

a. by the workers of the Planned Economy.

b. through taxation only if other economic forms manage to ensure that unemployed citizens necessarily move into the Social Villages.

4 The amount of Tax-funded transfer payments depends on the inflow statistics into the Planned Economy for reasons of social need.

5 The social benefits of the Ministry of Planned Economy are covered in case of emergency in addition to a share of 1% from the business taxes of all economic forms as the entrepreneur share and 1% of the value added tax as the consumer share. The tax rates are adjusted by the law to the prevailing facts.

§231[430] Integration of disabled persons[431]

1 The Ministry of Labour *promotes the inclusion of* disabled people with chronic illnesses or disabilities through referrals to the Ministries of Planned Economy and Social Market Economy.

2 The Ministry of Planned Economy *promotes the inclusion of disabled persons, especially through the construction and operation of institutions for housing and work.*

---

430 BV Art. 112b

431 Ministry of Labour - 12.1.2.2 Disabled people, Ministry of Social Market Economy - 6.6 Inclusion of disabled people, Ministry of Planned Economy - 18.1.6 House for disabled people

3 The Ministry of Social Market Economy sets out the objectives of inclusion *and the principles and criteria* that apply to companies in this economic form.

§232[432] Occupational pension scheme[433]

1 The Ministry of Labour, in voting with the ministries of economy, shall *issue regulations on occupational pension schemes.*
2 It shall *observe the following principles:*
a. The occupational benefit scheme, together with social security, enables the continuation of *the (...) way of life in a* self-determined manner.
b. Occupational pension provision is compulsory for workers in the Social Market Economy, and voluntary in the Barter Economy and Free Market Economy. *The law may provide for exceptions.*
c. The Ministry of Labour offers a Citizens' Insurance in which all contributions from citizens or from occupational pension funds of all economic forms are paid in, saved and earn interest. This Citizens' Insurance is compulsory for switching between economic forms in the course of a working life inland.
3 The Ministry of Planned Economy provides basic supply for domestic nationals who have inadequate private and occupational provision.

§233[434] Unemployment placement[435]

1 The Ministry of Labour shall issue *regulations on the placement of* unemployed persons.

---

432 BV Art. 113
433 Ministry of Labour - 10.2.4 Citizens' Insurance, Ministry of Free Market Economy - 14.2.4.2 Pensions, Ministry of Social Market Economy - 17.5.3 Unemployment Insurance, Ministry of Planned Economy - 17.1 Social Welfare, Ministry of Barter Economy - 9 Enterprise Policy
434 BV Art.114
435 Ministry of Labour - 12.2.1 Employment Exchange, Ministry of Planned Economy - 10.6 Innovation Enterprise, 10.8 Experimental Enterprise, 10.8.2 Start-up Fund, 17.2 Social Emergency

2 It shall observe the following principles:
a. All companies must publish their vacancies in the Labour Directory.
b. All state educational institutions create conditions for the immediate start of classes in all specialist departments with labour shortages. To this end, the Ministry of Education receives information on affected specialist departments from the Ministry of Labour.
c. Start-ups can be supported by the Ministries of Planned Economy and Innovation.
d. All residents of the Social Villages are provided with adequate opportunities to view residents' expertise, to come together, to bring new products or services to market, to start operations and, once profitable, to continue these companies in other economic forms.
3 The Ministry of Planned Economy operates a Start-up Fund to promote business start-ups in the Social Villages.
4 The Social Villages keep free housing for social emergencies and an emergency service for immediate move to the nearest Social Village.

§234[436] Children's rights, child benefit and parental protection[437]

1 The Ministry of Family Affairs shall take into account *the needs of the family in the performance of its duties.* It may implement and *support measures to protect the family.*
2 It shall issue *regulations on* children's rights and ensure that they are observed.
3 It pays the child benefit into a children's account at the People's Bank. All third-party care services are paid with child benefit as a priority. It pays a monthly contribution of 1% of the child benefit into the personal state pension fund. The

---

436 BV Art. 116
437 Ministry of Family Affairs - 7 Families, 7.5.3 Birth, 7.5.4 Parental leave, 8.1 Children's rights, 8.4 Child benefits, Ministry of Free Market Economy - 6.2 Duties on companies, Ministry of Social Market Economy - 6.8 Childcare, 17.5.2 Parental insurance, Ministry of Planned Economy - 9.3.8 Parental protection, Ministry of Barter Economy - 16.3 Child welfare

remainder can be spent by parents and guardians for the benefit of the child to pay for goods and services for the child with the child benefit.[438]

4 The ministries of family and economy shall issue regulations for parental protection.

5 The Ministry of Social Market Economy offers parental insurance.

§235[439] Health and accident insurance[440]

1 The Ministry of Health shall issue *regulations on health and accident insurance.*

2 It operates the Addictive Drugs Health Insurance and Immortality Health Insurance schemes.

3 It operates the general health insurance, which is a compulsory insurance in the social market economy.

4 Accident insurance is a compulsory insurance for companies that employ staff.

§236[441] Healthcare[442]

1 The Ministry of Health protects and promotes *health.* It supports sufficient *and economically viable medical and nursing care for the population*.

2 It shall ensure coordination with *private institutions*.

3 It promotes help *and care at home* and supports effective measures in the field of *addiction prevention*, as well as *natural healing methods.*

4 It shall *supervise the* state *and private institutions, the health*

---

438 Ministry of Finance
439 BV Art. 117
440 Ministry of Labour - 14.2 Occupational safety and health, Ministry of Health - 5.12 Health insurance, Ministry of Social Market Economy - 17.5.1 Health insurance
441 KV Art.41, BV Art. 117a
442 Ministry of Health - 4, 4.4.2 Health risks, 4.5, 5.2 3 Health Directory, 5.4.1 Licensing, 5.4.1.3 Healers, 5.5 Medical Fee Schedule, 5.6 Health Facilities, 5.7.10 Pharmaceutical Industry, 5.12 Health Insurance, 5.12.3 Addictive drugs Health Insurance, Ministry of Social Market Economy - 17.5.1 Health Insurance, Ministry of Planned Economy - 11.1.4 Health, 18.1.3 Health Centre

<u>*professions and the therapeutic products sector.*</u>
5 The *Ministry of Health shall issue regulations on:*
a. *education and training for basic supply professions and on the*
requirements for practising these professions;
b. *the appropriate remuneration for* medical *services*;
c. all things that endanger health and the environment.
6 It ensures the high quality of all medical services in state <u>*and*</u>
<u>*private institutions,*</u> the health <u>*professions and*</u> the <u>*remedies sector*</u>
through a Health Card, the Health Register and the health
auditors of the Company Auditing Agency.
7 The Health Card contains all the examination results of an
insured person or the admission to the storage location.
8 The health register contains all diagnoses, treatments and
medications of all doctors whose success rate can be rated by
the patients treated.
9 The Ministry of Health, in voting with the Ministries of
Planned Economy and Social Market Economy, shall ensure
sufficient *(...) basic supply of high quality.*
10 Admission to state medical care is reserved for domestic
nationals in the planned economy and for all workers in the
social market economy.

§237[443] **Protection of health and the environment[444]**

1 The Ministry of Health shall take measures *to protect health*
and the environment within the scope of its responsibilities.
2 It shall *issue regulations on:*
a. *the handling of foodstuffs as well as medicines, narcotics,*
organisms, chemicals and objects which may endanger health;
b. *the control of communicable, highly prevalent or malignant*
diseases of humans and animals;
c. *protection against ionising radiation*, noise and pollution;
d. the purity, production and trade of narcotic drugs and
medicines.

---

443 BV Art. 118
444 Ministry of Health - 4 Healthcare system, 4.1 Health Agency, 5.5
Medical Fee Schedule, 5.9 Medicines, 5.11 Drugs, 6.3 Food Safety, 6.4
Product Safety, 6.5 Sustainable Use of Nature

§238[445] Alternative medicine[446]

1 The Ministry of Health shall ensure that alternative medicine is taken into *account within the scope of* its responsibilities.
2 It ensures equal participation in the health directory for the quality control of medical services.

§239[447] Research on humans[448]

1 The Ministry of Health shall *enact* laws on research involving human beings insofar as *the protection* of human *dignity and (...) personality so requires. In so doing,* it shall safeguard *freedom of research and take account of the importance of research for health and society.*
2 *For research (...) with persons,* it shall observe *the following principles:*
a. *Every research project requires that the persons participating or entitled according to the law have given their informed consent. (...) Refusal is binding in all cases.*
b. *The risks and burdens for the participating persons must not be disproportionate to the benefits of the research project.*
c. *A research project may only be carried out with persons incapable of judgement if equivalent findings cannot be obtained with persons capable of judgement. If the research project does not lead to any direct benefit for the person lacking capacity, the risks and burdens may only be minimal.* Incapacity must be justified by the individual's state of health.
d. *A (...) review of the research project* by the medical service of the Company Auditing Agency *must have shown that the protection of the participating persons is guaranteed.*
e. The Company Auditing Agency's medical service monitors compliance with these principles as part of its regular company audits.

---

445 BV Art. 118a
446 Ministry of Health - 5.3 Health Directory, 5.4.1.3 Healers, 5.9 Medicines
447 BV Art. 118b
448 Ministry of Health - 4.3 Health Committee, 4.4.1 Damage limitation, 4.4.2 Health risks, 5.4.2.1 Medical research, 5.10 Pharmaceutical industry

§240[449] Reproductive medicine and genetic engineering in the human sector[450]

1 Humans are protected from abuses of reproductive medicine and genetic engineering.
2 The Ministry of Health shall *enact laws in voting with the people* and the Ethics Commission on the handling of *human germinal and genetic material.*
3 It shall *ensure the protection of human dignity, the person and the family.* It shall *observe the following principles in particular:*
a. Voluntary and unpaid surrogacy and sperm donation is permitted.
b. The genetic material *of a person may only be removed, examined, registered or disclosed if the person affected consents or if the law so requires.*
c. *Every person shall have admission to the data concerning his or her parentage.*

§241[451] Transplant medicine[452]

1 The Ministry of Health shall issue *regulations in the field of organ, tissue and cell transplantation.* It shall ensure the *protection of human dignity, personality and health.*
2 In particular, it shall *lay down criteria for the equitable allocation of organs.*
3 The donation of human organs, tissues and cells is free of charge. The trade in human organs is prohibited unless they have been artificially cultured.
4 All nationals are organ donors as long as they do not object and this information is recorded on the Health Card.

---

449 BV Art. 119
450 Ministry of Health - 4.3 Health Committee, 4.4.1 Damage limitation, 5.4.2.2 Reproduction
451 BV Art. 119a
452 Ministry of Health - 5.2 Health Card, 5.4.2.3 Transplantation, 5.10 Pharmaceutical Industry

§242[453] Genetic engineering in the non-human sector[454]

1 Humans and their environment are protected from the late effects and *abuses of genetic engineering.*
2 The Ministry of Health shall issue *regulations on the handling of germinal and genetic material of animals, plants and other organisms. In doing so,* it shall take into account *the dignity of creation and the safety of humans, animals and the environment and shall protect the genetic diversity of animal and plant species.*
3 It controls the isolated breeding of genetically modified animals and plants. In particular, it prevents genetically modified inheritance and germinal material from entering the environment.

Chapter 10: Residence and Settlement of Foreigners

§243[455] Legislation on foreigners and asylum[456]

1 Legislation on the entry and departure, residence and settlement of foreigners as well as on the granting of asylum is the responsibility of the Ministry of Integration in voting with the Ministry of Foreign Affairs.
2 Foreigners are expelled *from* the inland *if they endanger the security of the country.*
3 Irrespective of their status under aliens law, they lose their right of residence and all legal claims to residence in inland if they:
a. have been sentenced to a custodial sentence or three lesser sentences by *a final court decision; or*
b. have improperly received social insurance benefits or social welfare.
4 The Ministry of Justice shall define the facts in accordance with *paragraph 3 in more detail.* The Ministry of Integration may add *further offences.*

---

453 BV Art. 120
454 Ministry of Health - 6.4 Product Safety, 6.5.6 Genetic Engineering
455 BV Art. 121
456 Ministry of Foreign Affairs - 4.7.3.4 Visas, 4.7.3.6 Deportations, 9 Asylum application procedures, Ministry of Integration - 7 Immigration, 7.9.3 Deportations, 8 Asylum, 8.4.2 Responsibilities, Ministry of Justice - 8.9.4 Deportations

5 Foreigners who lose their right of residence and all legal rights to reside inland in accordance with paragraphs 3 and 4 shall be immediately deported *by* authorities of the Ministry of Security *and banned from entering the country for* life.
6 Anyone who disregards the entry ban or (...) enters the inland illegally is liable to prosecution. The Ministry of Justice shall issue the corresponding laws in voting with the Ministry of Integration.

§244[457] Immigration management[458]

1 The domestic people manage *the immigration of foreigners independently.*

2 The number of permits for the residence of foreigners inland is determined by a quota of foreigners in the constitution, which is determined by referendum. The quota of foreigners may be changed by a quorum. Municipal exceptions are permitted if they do not exceed the national maximum numbers and quotas. *The maximum numbers apply to all permits under the law on foreigners, including asylum.*

3 The *entitlement to permanent residence* and *to family reunification may be restricted.*

4 Social benefits are excluded for foreigners, admission to the Barter Economy and Planned Economy is only granted after payment of entrance fees. Only asylum seekers are supported by social benefits. Details are regulated by the Ministry of Integration in voting with the Ministries of Infrastructure and Planned Economy.

5 The annual maximum numbers and quotas for gainfully employed foreigners shall be geared to the overall economic and public welfare *interests* of the country, taking into account *a priority for domestic* nationals. *The cross-border commuters are to be included.*

6 The decisive *criteria for the granting of residence permits are the application of an employer, the ability to integrate and a sufficient, independent livelihood.* The Ministry of Integration

---

457 BV Art. 121a
458 Ministry of Integration - 7.4 Quota of foreigners, 7.5 Conditions of immigration, 7.5.1 Entry conditions for economic forms, 7.5.2 Guest work, 8 Asylum, 8.4.2 Responsibilities

stipulates more details on the ability to integrate in the law.
7 A second quota of foreigners may be instituted for nationals of states with which the inland is in an International Union.

§245 Quota of foreigners[459]

1 Foreigners from third countries may make up a maximum of 5% of the total population of the country.
2 Foreigners from Continental Union member states may make up a maximum of 20% of the country's total population.

§246[460] Naturalisation[461]

1 Foreigners can be naturalised, which gives them the statistical right to vote and an unlimited residence permit.
2 The Ministry of Integration shall enact laws on naturalisation.
3 The residence permit shall not be issued to or withdrawn from a foreigner who:
a. has been convicted of a crime by a final court decision;
b. Receives benefits from social welfare or has not fully repaid benefits received;
c. does not have a proven good knowledge of the *official language;*
d. does not have proven knowledge of national and *municipal* legislation *and its history;*
e. does not have sufficient means to provide for himself and his dependants.
4 A foreigner is granted a permanent residence permit if he or she loves, marries and does not divorce a person with domestic nationality or who was fathered by at least one person with domestic nationality.
5 National citizenship is granted to anyone who is fathered by at least one person with domestic nationality.
6 Children where only one parent has domestic nationality are

---

459 Ministry of Integration - 7.4 Quota of foreigners, 7.4.1 Voting questionnaire for nationals
460 KV Art.7
461 Ministry of Integration - 4.1 Nationals, 4.2.3 Naturalised foreigners, 4.2.3.1 Naturalisation test, 7.5 Immigration conditions, 7.7 Integration measures

given the nationality of the foreign parent. They can opt for domestic nationality from the age of ten and until they reach the age of majority.

Chapter 11: State law, civil law, criminal law, metrology

§247[462] State law[463]

1 Legislation in the field of state law is the responsibility of the Ministry of State Organisation in voting with affected ministries.
2 State cases are administrative proceedings concerning services that state agencies or citizens are legally obliged to provide or are legally entitled to.
3 The Ministry of Justice shall legislate on court proceedings in state law. The Ministry of State Organisation undertakes legislation on mediation, executive and legislation in state law and state procedural law.
4 The Ministry of Justice takes measures *to enforce* international, national and municipal law.

§248[464] Civil law[465]

1 Legislation in the field of civil law and civil procedure is the responsibility of the Ministry of Justice.
2 The Municipal Courts are responsible for the organisation of court proceedings *and the jurisprudence in civil matters at* first instance.

---

462 BV Art.173
463 Ministry of Justice - 4.8.3 State Law, 5.4 Courts, Ministry of State Organisation - 4 State Law, 4.1 State Procedure Law
464 BV Art. 122
465 Ministry of Justice - 4.8.1 Civil law, 5.4.3 Municipal Courts

§249[466] Criminal law[467]

1 Legislation in the field of criminal law and criminal procedure is the responsibility of the Ministry of Justice.
2 The Municipal Courts are responsible for the first instance organisation of court proceedings and *the jurisprudence in criminal cases.*
3 The Ministry of Justice is responsible for the execution of sentences and measures, *unless the law provides otherwise.* It shall issue *regulations on the execution of sentences and measures.* Specifically for:
a. the establishment of prisons;
b. Training, further training and, if possible, therapy *in the penal system and in the correctional system;*
c. Institutions that carry out educational measures on children, youths and young adults.
4 *In the assessors' reports required for the court judgment,* violent offenders who are considered *extremely dangerous and cannot be treated* are *to be* imprisoned for the rest of their lives due *to* a *high risk of recidivism. Early release and furlough are excluded.*
5 *Only if new, scientific findings prove that* offenders can *be cured and thus no longer* pose *a danger to the public, new expert reports can be drawn up. If custody is lifted on the basis of these new reports, the liability for a recidivism of the offender must be assumed by* the agency that lifted the custody.
6 *All assessors for the assessment of (...) violent offenders shall be prepared by at least* three *experienced experts who are independent of each other, taking into account all the bases that are important for the assessment.*
7 A limitation period of 20 years applies to criminal offences.
8 There is no statute of limitations for prosecution for murder, other homicide offences as well as for rape offences against minors.
9 *Persons convicted of interfering with the (...) integrity of a child or a dependent person definitively lose the right to engage in professional or honorary service with minors or dependents.*

466BV Art. 123, 123a, 123c
467Ministry of Justice - 4.8 Areas of law, 4.8.2 Criminal law, 5 Court proceedings, 5.4.3 Municipal Courts, 7.3 Occupational ban, 7.5 Detention, 7.5.2 Assessment of detention period

§250[468] Victim assistance[469]

1 The Ministry of Justice shall ensure *that persons whose physical, psychological or sexual integrity has been impaired by a criminal offence receive assistance and adequate compensation.*
2 The costs are borne by offenders. If this is not possible, the Ministry of Justice spends tax money. This amount must be worked off by insolvent offenders during detention.

§251[470] Duration of detention[471]

1 Unless the law provides otherwise, the damage caused is quantified in monetary value according to information from the insurance industry and converted into hours of imprisonment.
2 Prisoners are remunerated per hour in detention at the Social Market Economy minimum wage. This gives an hourly detention rate based on the currently applicable minimum wage and the damage caused.
3 The assets generated by prisoners during detention shall be sufficient to finance detention and compensate victims. Surpluses flow into the state budget of the following year.
4 The people issue *pardons and decide on amnesty* in a committee with subsequent voting.

§252[472] Metrology[473]

Legislation on metrology and the determination of units of measurement *is the responsibility of the Ministry of Labour in voting with* the Ministry of Education.

---

468 BV Art. 124
469 Ministry of Justice - 4.8.2 Criminal law
470 BV Art. 173
471 Ministry of Justice - 6 Clemency law, 7.5.2 Assessment of detention period, 7.5.10 Labour
472 BV Art. 125
473 Ministry of Labour - 20.10 Institute for Evaluation

Title 6: Amendment of the Constitution and Transitional Provisions

Chapter 1: Amendments to the Constitution

§253[474] Constitutional amendments[475]

1 The Constitution may *be amended in whole or in part* by the people at *any time.*
2 Where the Constitution *and the legislation based on it do not provide otherwise, the amendment shall follow the* same procedure of the committees and voting of direct democratic *legislation.* Counter-drafts or counter-templates are possible.
3 This Constitution shall cease to be valid on the day on which the people vote in favour of a total or partial revision and thus have a new Constitution.

§254[476] Total revision[477]

1 A total revision of the constitution may *be* demanded *by the people by means of a revision quorum.*
2 If the initiative is a suggestion or a draft, the Ministry of State Organisation shall convene a constitutional committee per constitutional article to prepare a template for a new constitution. Once templates for all articles have been prepared, a constitutional referendum is scheduled by the Ministry of State Organisation.
3 If the initiative is a template, a constitutional referendum shall be scheduled by the Ministry of State Organisation to vote on the template for a new constitution.
4 A constitutional referendum on a total revision shall be held at least every 50 years. If there is no initiative, the current constitutional text is put to a constitutional referendum. If it is rejected, a constitutional committee shall be convened.

---

474 BV Art. 192
475 Ministry of State Organisation - 9.6.2.3 Mandatory Committees, 9.7.4 Mandatory Voting, 9.11 Constitutional Amendments
476 BV Art. 193
477 Ministry of State Organisation - 9.11.4 Total revision

§255[478] Partial revision[479]

1 A partial revision of the Constitution may *be demanded by the people by means of* a revision quorum for each individual article *(...)*.
2 A <u>*partial revision may amend one or more substantively related provisions of the Constitution.*</u>
3 If the initiative is a suggestion or a draft, a constitutional committee shall be convened by the Ministry of State Organisation to prepare a template for one or more new or amended articles. Once the article or articles have been drafted, the Ministry of State Organisation shall schedule a constitutional referendum.
4 If the initiative is a template, a constitutional referendum shall be scheduled by the Ministry of State Organisation to vote on the article(s).
5 The (...) partial revision must also preserve the unity of the constitution.

§256 Revision quorum[480]

1 In order to open a revision quorum, a constitutional initiative must be introduced.
2 2% of those entitled to vote may, by means of a revision quorum, demand the amendment of an article of the Constitution or introduce an initiative for a new article.
3 10% of those entitled to vote may, by means of a revision quorum, demand the amendment of several articles of the Constitution or submit initiatives for several new articles.
4 25% of those entitled to vote may demand the revision of the entire constitution by means of a revision quorum and submit an initiative for a new constitution.
5 Any revision quorum met shall, in the case of a suggestion or draft, first trigger a constitutional committee and then a constitutional referendum. A constitutional referendum is held immediately on a template.

---

478 BV Art. 194, KV Art.128
479 Ministry of State Organisation - 9.11.3 Partial revision
480 Ministry of State Organisation - 9.5.16 Revision quorum

§257[481] Constitutional initiative[482]

1 *The constitutional* initiative may take the form of a *general suggestion, a draft or an elaborated* template. It may concern individual, several or all articles of the constitution, which are to be amended, abolished or newly inserted. Suggestions and drafts are formulated into templates in a constitutional committee. Templates are put directly to a constitutional referendum.

2 Citizens can submit constitutional initiatives to the deputy ministers of state organisation in their municipality, opening a revision quorum.

3 Counter-drafts may be introduced up to the beginning of the Constitutional Committee. Counter-templates may be introduced until the beginning of the election week for the constitutional referendum. Counter-drafts and counter-templates must have been supported by 1% of those entitled to vote in another revision quorum in order to also be admitted to the constitutional committee or constitutional referendum.

4 The political parties are responsible for giving advice to the initiators on how the text could be proposed in order to preserve the unity of the constitution and international law.

5 If the initiative violates the unity of *form, the unity of the* constitution *or international law*, a counter-template shall be prepared in the Constitutional Committee. The counter-template must correspond as far as possible to the core content of the initiative without violating the rest of the constitution or international law.

6 If international law is violated in an amended constitution, the Ministry of Foreign Affairs is instructed to renegotiate or terminate the relevant treaty under international law.

7 If an initiative violates the rest of the constitution, it must be discussed in a committee together with all affected articles. Templates can only be put to a constitutional referendum if, if approved, the constitution remains unopposed.

8 Constitutional initiatives must not violate mandatory

---

481 BV Art. 139

482 Ministry of State Organisation - 9.11.1 Constitutional initiative, 9.11.1.1 Reviews, 9.11.1.2 Counter-initiative, 9.11.1.3 Counter-template by Constitutional Committee

provisions of international law. These are non-violence with the right to defence, protection of the environment for descendants and respect for human rights.

§258 Constitutional referendum[483]

1 The constitutional referendum shall decide on the amendment or repeal of an article, several articles or the entire constitution.
2 As soon as several articles or the entire constitution are put to the vote, those entitled to vote shall be given the opportunity to accept or reject all articles individually.
3 In constitutional referendums, voting is compulsory for all domestic citizens living in the inland.

§259[484] Entry into force[485]

1 *The constitution, as* amended in *whole or in part, shall enter into force when it has been adopted by the people by a* majority of at least 80%.
2 *If new law is to be enacted under this Constitution, this must be done without delay.*

Chapter 2: Transitional Provisions

§260[486] Transitional provisions

1 Transitional provisions are more precise and detailed provisions for articles of the Constitution to assist subsequent legislation. Initially, the article to which the transitional provision refers shall be mentioned.
2 The procedure for enacting transitional provisions shall correspond to that for a partial revision of the Constitution.

---

483 Ministry of State Organisation - 9.11.5 Constitutional referendum, 9.11.5.1 Compulsory voting in constitutional referendums
484 BV Art. 195, KV Art.133
485 Ministry of State Organisation - 9.11.5 Constitutional referendum
486 BV Art.196

§261 Transitional provision towards this constitution[487]

This is a transitional provision to Article 254 Total Revision
1 The existing constitution shall continue to apply until the new constitution has been adopted in a referendum. For this purpose, a constitutional committee is convened to draft the first and subsequently all further articles of the new constitution.
2 The draft used is this constitution of the dynamic media democracy. The Constitution of the Swiss Confederation and the Constitution of the Canton of Bern serve as aids.
3 Each article shall be negotiated in turn in a constitutional committee and adopted or rejected in a constitutional referendum.
4 This constitutional process may not last longer than 4 years. The constitutional referendum shall be divided into several votes.
5 The articles are discussed before the Constitutional Committee on the internet on the Constitutional Court's website by nationals. In accordance with the "Solution Finder" concept, suggestions for improvement can be made, commented on and rated. At the committees, these proposals are then included in the negotiations. At the end of a committee, the finalised text of the constitutional article is submitted to the people for voting in the following election week.
6 Each article is acted out on stage by a committee of actors. An article up for constitutional referendum will be filmed, broadcast and stored for public access before the election week. During the film, the wording of the filmed scene is inserted in the subtitle.
7 The Ministry of State Organisation regulates the transition of state law to this constitution in law.

---

487 Ministry of State Organisation - 13.1 Amendment of the Constitution

Contact form

Dear reader
If you would like to make what you have read come true, in whole or in part, together with other like-minded people, I offer you several possibilities with this contact form. Fill it out, tear out the page and send it by post to:
Andreas Seidl, P.O. Box 1206, 63488 Seligenstadt / Germany

Or send the details to:
Phone: 0049 1522 818 2243 (whatsapp, telegram, signal)
Email: andreas.seidl2022@web.de

Please mark with a cross:
O   I want to found a dynamic People's Party.
O   I want to donate money for implementation.
O   I want contacts with like-minded people in my area.

Forename: ___________________________________

Surname: ___________________________________

Please fill in only the contact option through which a reply should be made.

Street, house no.: ___________________________________

Postcode, city, country: ___________________________________

Phone: ___________________________________

Email address: ___________________________________